FEED ME VEGAN

Lucy Watson

FEED ME VEGAN

sphere

Contents

Introduction

Welcome to my cookbook!

Whether you are vegan, vegetarian, or just a serious lover of food then I can't wait for you to dive in and indulge yourself with some of these delicious recipes. This is a book that will suit everyone – and it was all started when I went vegan nearly two years ago.

There's a common misconception that vegans eat just salad or vegetables, something I struggled with when I first made the transition. I've always loved food but I was willing to sacrifice the pleasures of eating delicious meals in order to stop contributing to animal cruelty. Until I realised that I didn't need to! I spent months trying out new recipes and looking for alternatives to all my favourite meals when I made the switch. People repeatedly ask me 'but if you're vegan, what do you eat?' and that was why I decided I had to create this book.

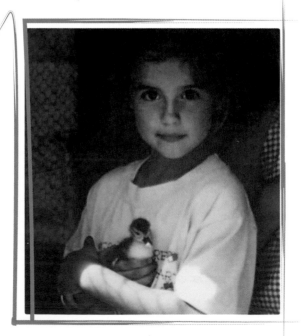

My love of animals and dislike of eating meat started when I was just six years old. Growing up on a farm, I would feed the ducks every morning and when lambing time came around we even helped deliver the lambs. Occasionally the sheep would reject their lambs and then we were allowed to hand rear them ourselves until they were big enough to rejoin the herd, which was magical. I loved all the animals around me as much as the dogs that lived in our home. To me, there was no difference and I became unable to ignore the connection between what was on my plate and who was playing in my fields – my mum can clearly recall mealtimes where I would clamp my mouth shut, shake my head and refuse to eat meat.

I completely rebelled against meat-eating after my favourite lamb, Maisie, was sent off to slaughter. The experience was so life changing for me that from that day forward I stopped eating meat. I couldn't bear the idea of eating the living beings I watched being carted off in large lorries every few months, memories that I still find traumatising to think of now and impossible to remove from my mind.

Having lived most of my life as a vegetarian, as I got older and became more educated about other industries inflicting cruelty on animals it became clear to me that veganism was the only way forward. For other vegans, the catalyst may be becoming aware of the massive contribution the meat and dairy industries make to carbon emissions around the world, and realising that a vegan diet has the smallest carbon footprint. Others turn to veganism for health reasons – not only can you lower your cholesterol and increase your energy levels but you can also improve your health overall.

For all those reasons, whenever I get asked 'why are you vegan?' (which is often) my response is always, 'why NOT?' It's not only the lives of animals you'll be saving by becoming vegan, but you will help to save the planet and maybe even yourself.

Feed Me Vegan is here to smash any negative mis-conceptions about vegan diets and show people just how diverse and delicious vegan food can be: how to easily whip up a vegan burger a meat-eater would be happy to wolf down, make the perfect vegan mac and cheese to comfort eat on rainy winter nights, or even bake a decadent chocolate cake to satisfy any sweet tooth! There are quick and easy ways of making all your favourite meals guilt-free, without any of those 'sacrifices' that people dread when contemplating becoming vegan.

All in all there really is no downside to veganism . . . I know that there's definitely no going back for me. Once you inform yourself about the cruelty inherent in these heavily marketed industries, it doesn't feel right to continue your life with them in it. Although it can sometimes be hard not to just 'fit in' and eat what's there because it's 'easier', I promise you it's all worthwhile.

Now get stuck in and enjoy the recipes, with a completely clean conscience! Love,

Lucy
x

STORE *Cupboard*

A good selection of herbs and spices is essential in any kitchen cupboard, but for vegan meals it really will make all the difference to your cooking, and ensure that what you make is just as tasty as anything you ate before you made the switch. The herbs and spices you'll really want to keep your cupboard stocked with are:

Bay leaves
Cardamom
Cinnamon
Cumin
Curry powder
Fennel
Fenugreek
Garam masala

Ginger
Italian herbs
Mustard seeds
Oregano
Paprika
Rosemary
Sage
Sea Salt
Turmeric

Chia seeds

Paprika

As well as these, here are a few other essentials I'd recommend as they can be great for adding to a variety of different recipes:

Agave syrup
Chia seeds
Cacao nibs
Coconut oil
Egg replacer – a great friend for vegan baking!
Hickory liquid smoke – perfect for adding that smoky BBQ flavour
Liquid aminos – this similar to soy sauce, perfect for Asian-inspired recipes
Mirin – a Japanese rice wine, again brilliant for adding to Asian dishes
Nutritional yeast – nutty and creamy, essential for adding a cheesy flavour into dishes
White miso

There are many different vegan brands you can buy as alternatives to meat and dairy, and the ones you choose make a difference to how the food you cook ends up tasting. Through lots of trial and error I've narrowed down my favourites – they pack in all the flavour you'll need to make delicious meals. They are:

Protein powder: Sun Warrior
Vegan chocolate: Ombar or Booja Booja
Marshmallows: Freedom
Almond milk: Rude Health Ultimate Almond Drink
Soya milk: Waitrose own brand
Coconut cream: Biona
Soya cream, Vegan yogurt: Alpro
Vegan squirty cream: Soyatoo
Vegan ice cream: Booja Booja Swedish Glace Neapolitan
Vegan butter: Pure soya spread
Cheeses: Violife and Sheese are both great!
Vegan mayo: Vegenaise
Mince: Meat the Alternative
Vegan bacon: Vegideli or Mheat
Tofu (all kinds): Tofoo Co
Worcestershire sauce: Biona

Cacao Nibs

Nutritional Yeast

When it comes to *finding* all of these different replacement products, it can be tricky. But the good news is that the options have got much easier owing to the growth in independent stores stocking vegan food products. I would really recommend trying to find your own local vegan grocers, as supporting them is so important. If you don't have anything nearby, Wholefoods or Ocado online are brilliant, and Sainsbury's and Tesco also have a great (and growing!) selection of vegan products.

Another thing to do is make sure you check the labels of drinks like beer, wine and wine vinegars – most are vegan but you can occasionally be caught out because animal products have been used in processing. If in doubt, the internet is definitely your friend for double checking. The best place to start is www.barnivore.com – it has information on 32,000 different drinks!

Finally, here is a small selection of brands that you might not know are actually vegan: Oreos, (most) champagne, Skittles, Heinz Tomato Ketchup, Skips, Metcalfe's popcorn, Bourbon biscuits, Marmite and Jus-Rol Pastry. Check your favourite brands and snacks online – you could be surprised to find that some are vegan.

Feed Me
BREAKFAST

*A '*photo opportunity' *favourite of mine, I wanted to include this recipe as it's inspired by visits I have made to Bali. Gorgeous to look at, sweet to taste and surprisingly filling, you can top it with pretty much anything. I like it with kiwis and passion fruit, but there are no end of options so feel free to go wild – bright colours look the best!*

Mango Smoothie BOWL

SERVES 2

1 young coconut (100g flesh, 250ml coconut water)
2 bananas, cut into chunks and frozen
250g frozen ripe mango chunks
Juice of 1 lime
2 tbsp agave syrup

For the toppings:
1 passion fruit, halved
1 kiwi fruit, peeled and sliced
2 tbsp toasted coconut flakes
1 tbsp chia seeds
2 tbsp pomegranate seeds
2 tbsp nibbed pistachio nuts

Using a very sharp knife, cut across the top of the coconut, until you see a bit of white flesh poking through. Stab the exposed flesh with the tip of your knife. Continue to stab the top until you have made a large enough hole to lift up the top of the coconut. Pour the coconut water inside into a jug and lift the top of the coconut off. Using a spoon, scoop out all the lovely flesh from inside. Divide the flesh into two – keep half for decoration.

Prepare all your topping ingredients before you blend the smoothie.

To make the smoothie, put the coconut water, half the coconut flesh, the banana, frozen mango, lime juice and agave into a powerful blender or food processor. Blend until completely smooth. If the mixture is too thick, add some water or coconut water to loosen it.

Spoon the mixture into two serving bowls and add the toppings, including the rest of the coconut. Serve immediately.

A sweet and healthy smoothie to brighten up your morning. Spinach is very nutritious and the pineapple helps to balance out its mild bitterness – you really won't be able to pinpoint the spinach flavour. Smoothies like this one are quick and easy to make, and help to fill you with some of the valuable nutrients we all need.

Pineapple & Spinach SMOOTHIE

SERVES 2

4 Granny Smith apples
½ cucumber
1 lime, peeled
100g baby spinach leaves
1 handful of mint leaves
150g frozen pineapple
1 small handful of ice cubes

Pass the apple, cucumber and lime through an electric juicer. Put the juice into a powerful blender with the remaining ingredients. Blend for at least 1 minute or until the mixture is completely smooth. Pour into serving glasses and enjoy!

This is one of the recipes that I knew I had to nail after making the transition to veganism. I definitely prefer (but try hard to refrain from) sweet breakfasts. I was literally raised on pancakes – my mum made them for me and my sister every day before school! Having a good pancake recipe in my life will always be pretty much essential. For this version, the banana replaces the egg and gives you that creamy mixture to work with. They may not look like what you're used to but, trust me, they're delicious.

Banana & Buckwheat PANCAKES

SERVES 2

2 ripe bananas
125g buckwheat flour
150g wholemeal plain flour
1 tsp baking powder
½ tsp ground cinnamon
1 tsp vanilla extract
2 tbsp maple syrup
180ml almond milk
2 tbsp coconut oil

To serve:
1 banana, sliced
80g blueberries
Pancake syrup or maple syrup

Peel the bananas and put them into a large bowl. Mash the bananas with a fork until creamy. Sift in the flours, baking powder and cinnamon, and stir well, then add the vanilla extract and maple syrup. Stir well to combine. Whisk in the milk until you have a thick, smooth batter.

Put two non-stick frying pans over a medium heat. Divide the coconut oil between the two pans. Using a ladle, pour 3 ladlefuls of batter into each pan to make 3 pancakes. Allow these to cook gently for 2–3 minutes on one side until bubbling, then flip them over and cook for a further 2–3 minutes until thick and fluffy.

Put 3 pancakes onto each serving plate. Serve topped with the sliced banana and blueberries, and drizzled with pancake syrup.

Porridge is so quick and easy to make, but, let's be honest, it can be a tad bland. Luckily, there are so many different ways that you can make it more exciting – my favourite is adding some chocolate protein powder. Though I wouldn't eat it every morning, this is the ideal fix for those mornings when you wake up and crave something sweet.

Chocolate PORRIDGE

SERVES 1

80g rolled oats
1 tbsp vegan chocolate
    protein powder
1 tbsp maple syrup
350ml chocolate almond milk

For the topping:
2 strawberries, halved
1 tbsp toasted hazelnuts,
    roughly chopped
1 tsp cacao nibs
1 tsp light muscovado sugar

Put the oats in a small non-stick saucepan. Add the remaining ingredients to the pan, stir well and put over a medium heat. Bring up to a gentle simmer and cook for 6–8 minutes until the oats are cooked and the mixture has thickened.

Spoon the chocolate porridge into a serving bowl. Serve topped with the strawberries, hazelnuts, cacao nibs and muscovado sugar.

The ultimate breakfast option for those out there with a sweet tooth like mine. As the traditional way of making French toast is to dip bread into egg and milk it might seem that it would be off-menu for vegans, but this alternative is surprisingly easy to create and just as scrummy. The spiced plums really do make it, though of course you can have it with any topping of your choice!

FRENCH TOAST *with Spiced Plums*

SERVES 2

200ml almond milk
2 tbsp light brown soft sugar
2 tbsp wholemeal flour
1 tbsp nutritional yeast
½ tsp ground cinnamon
A pinch of salt
2 tbsp vegan butter
4 thick slices day-old white
    bloomer bread, sliced about
    2cm thick

For the spiced plums:
3 tbsp vegan butter
3 tbsp light soft brown sugar
6 large ripe plums, pitted
    and quartered
¼ tsp ground ginger
¼ tsp ground cinnamon

Begin by pan-frying the plums. Put the butter and sugar in a non-stick frying pan over a high heat. When it begins to bubble, put the plums into the pan. Sprinkle over the spices and cook for 4–5 minutes until soft, stirring occasionally. The plums should be well coated with the glossy syrup. Remove from the heat.

Pour the milk into a bowl and add the sugar, flour, nutritional yeast, cinnamon and salt. Whisk well.

Put a large non-stick frying pan over a medium-high heat. Put the butter in the pan and wait until it begins to sizzle. Take each piece of bread and dip both sides into the milk mixture until soaked well.

Add the soaked bread slices to the pan and cook for 3–4 minutes on each side until golden brown and crispy. Put the plums back over the heat to warm through.

Serve the plums on the bread, making sure to use up all the spiced buttery syrup.

A nother sweet breakfast – because you can never have enough! I love these waffles with berries and vegan yogurt.

WAFFLES WITH Berries & Yogurt

SERVES 2

100g plain flour
100g wholemeal flour
2 tsp baking powder
3 tbsp golden caster sugar
1 tsp vanilla paste
A pinch of salt
250ml almond milk
4 tbsp vegan butter, melted

For the topping:
150g mixed berries
4 tbsp vegan strawberry and
    rhubarb yogurt

Sift the flours and baking powder into a bowl and add the sugar, vanilla paste and salt. Whisk in the milk until you have a smooth batter. Pour in half the melted butter and whisk again.

Preheat a waffle maker to High. Brush both the top and bottom of the waffle maker with some of the remaining melted butter. Ladle half the mixture into the waffle maker and press down the lid. Cook for 2–3 minutes until set and golden. Lift the lid and brush the top of the waffle with butter. Close the lid and cook for a further 2 minutes or until the top is golden and crispy. Remove from the waffle maker and put onto a plate. Repeat with the remaining batter.

Cut each waffle into four and serve topped with mixed berries and yogurt. Serve immediately.

I'm one of those people who always buys too many bananas and ends up with a few at that unappealing brown stage – but that's when they're PERFECT for banana bread. I've made some of my favourite banana bread batches since going vegan, and throwing some chocolate in there completes it. Ideal for on-the-go or as an indulgent sweet breakfast. It lasts for a few days in the fridge as well so don't feel like you need to eat it all straight away. Or you could – who's judging?!

Banana & Chocolate BREAD

MAKES 8–10 SLICES

70ml vegetable or light olive
   oil, plus extra for greasing
3 large very ripe bananas
100g soft light brown sugar
1 tsp ground cinnamon
200ml almond milk
300g plain flour
3 tbsp cocoa powder
3 tsp baking powder
½ tsp salt
100g walnuts or pecan nuts,
   chopped
150g vegan dark chocolate,
   roughly chopped

For the topping:
1 banana
2 tbsp soft light brown sugar

Preheat the oven to 200°C (180°C fan, gas 6) and grease a 900g loaf tin with a little oil.

Peel the bananas and put them into a large mixing bowl. Mash them well until they are creamy. Add the oil, sugar, cinnamon and milk. Combine well.

Sift in the flour, cocoa powder, baking powder and salt, then add the nuts and chocolate. Stir with a wooden spoon until all the ingredients have been incorporated. Pour the mixture into the prepared loaf tin.

Peel the banana and slice it lengthways. Lay both pieces on the loaf with the inside facing up. Sprinkle with sugar. Bake in the centre of the oven for 50–60 minutes until cooked through and a skewer inserted into the centre comes out clean. If there is cake mix on the skewer, return the loaf to the oven for 5–10 minutes more.

Leave it to cool in the tin for 5 minutes, then turn it out onto a wire rack to cool a little more. Slice and serve warm.

Pears and dates go so well together. If you haven't tried the combo before, you have to – you won't be disappointed! The moistness of the pear really complements the crumble topping, and the egg replacer helps these to be extra fluffy. I love baking, so if you're the same then you'll definitely have some fun with these.

Pear & Date CRUMBLE MUFFINS

MAKES 12

350g plain flour
2 tsp baking powder
1 tsp cinnamon
½ tsp salt
100g light muscovado sugar
50g golden caster sugar
100g pitted dried dates,
    finely chopped
2 tsp egg replacer
140ml soya milk
130g vegan butter, melted
400g can of pear halves in
    juice, drained and chopped
    into 1cm dice

For the crumble topping:
3 tbsp light muscovado sugar
2 tbsp golden caster sugar
2 tbsp plain flour
1 tbsp rolled oats, plus 2 tbsp
    to finish
½ tsp ground cinnamon
3 tbsp vegan butter, melted

Preheat the oven to 200°C (180°C fan, gas 6). Line a deep 12-cup muffin tray with paper muffin cases. Prepare the crumble topping by mixing the sugars in a small bowl. Add the flour, the 1 tbsp oats and the cinnamon.

Pour in half the melted butter and mix together with a fork. Pour in the remaining butter and mix again, until the mixture resembles large crumbs. Leave to one side.

To make the muffins, sift the flour, baking powder, cinnamon and salt into a large bowl. Add the sugars, stir well, then add the dates. Mix the egg replacer with 4 tsp water in a small bowl and add the milk and the melted butter, then whisk well. Add this mixture to the dry ingredients and stir well.

Add the pears and fold into the mixture gently. Divide the mixture among the muffin cases. Top each one with some crumble mixture and sprinkle each one with some of the extra rolled oats.

Bake for 25 minutes or until golden. Remove from the oven and leave to cool for a few minutes before devouring them.

A go-to of mine that everyone can enjoy! Avocados became my friends through becoming vegan, and I never get sick of them. Delicious with tomatoes, this is a bit of a classic these days. But make sure you catch your avocado in time! We all know they don't like to hang around for too long . . .

AVOCADO TOAST *with Tomatoes & Basil*

SERVES 1

½ ripe avocado, pitted

1 thick slice of sourdough
    bread, toasted

Juice of ½ lime

4 yellow cherry tomatoes,
    sliced

3 red cherry tomatoes,
    quartered

A few basil leaves

1 tbsp extra virgin olive oil

½ tsp balsamic vinegar

Sea salt and freshly ground
    black pepper

Scoop the flesh from the avocado using a tablespoon and slice it thinly. Gently press it down onto the toasted bread to create a fanned effect. Squeeze over the lime juice and season with salt and pepper.

Top with the cherry tomatoes and a little more salt and pepper. Add a few basil leaves, the olive oil and balsamic vinegar, then serve.

One of my simpler recipes: I think people forget how easy it is to make a vegan fry-up, which is why I've included it. Everyone loves a fry-up now and again – it's the perfect way to start a weekend – and this version is packed with different flavours. The smoked tofu is key to filling that 'meat' void.

Fry-UP

SERVES 2

150g potatoes, grated

2 tbsp vegan butter, melted

2 tsp nutritional yeast

1 tsp finely chopped flat-leaf
    parsley leaves

180g vine tomatoes

1 tsp olive oil, plus extra
    for frying

2 vegan sausages, thawed

100g smoked tofu, cut into
    4 slices

200g baked beans

1 ripe avocado, halved
    and pitted

2 slices of sourdough bread,
    toasted

Sea salt and freshly ground
    black pepper

Preheat the oven to 200°C (180°C fan, gas 6). To make röstis, squeeze any excess water from the grated potato; you want it to be as dry as possible. Put the grated potato in a small bowl. Pour over the melted butter and add the nutritional yeast and parsley. Season with a little salt and pepper, and mix well.

Put a small non-stick frying pan over a medium-high heat. When the pan is hot, divide the potato mixture into two portions and put both piles into the pan. Flatten each one down a little. Reduce the heat to medium and cook for 3–4 minutes on each side until golden brown.

Meanwhile, put the cherry tomatoes onto a baking tray, drizzle with a little olive oil and sprinkle with salt and pepper. Put into the oven. Put the pan with the röstis into the oven, and cook the tomatoes and the röstis for 10 minutes.

While they are cooking, heat a little olive oil in a medium frying pan and cook the sausages for 5 minutes. Add the tofu to the pan and cook for a further 2–3 minutes each side until golden.

Heat through the baked beans in a small pan over a medium heat. Scoop the flesh from the avocado using a tablespoon and slice it. Serve the tomatoes and röstis with the toast, avocado, sausages and tofu. Divide the baked beans into two small bowls and put onto the serving plates. Grab your favourite sauce and get stuck in!

A big fear when going vegan is that there'll be a lack of breakfast options as you won't be able to eat eggs. However, the egg industry is probably one of the cruellest, so a life without them is almost certainly a better one. Tofu scramble has become one of my favourite meals. Although tofu itself has very little flavour, cooking it the right way changes everything! It's healthy and nutritious and soon you'll forget why you loved eggs so much; I certainly have. Pile this high on a slice of toast with your favourite sauce.

Scrambled TOFU

SERVES 2

2 tbsp olive oil

½ onion, finely chopped

1 garlic clove, finely chopped

1cm piece of fresh root ginger, peeled and grated

½ tsp ground turmeric

100g chestnut mushrooms, thickly sliced

½ red pepper, deseeded and sliced

300g firm tofu, crumbled

1 tbsp nutritional yeast

1 tbsp soy sauce

1 handful of baby spinach

2 tbsp coriander or basil leaves, roughly chopped

1 handful of alfalfa sprouts

Sea salt and freshly ground black pepper

2 slices of your favourite bread, toasted

Heat a large non-stick frying pan over a medium heat. Add the oil and onion, and cook for 5 minutes or until softened and translucent. Put in the garlic and ginger, and cook for 2 minutes, then add the turmeric, mushrooms and pepper. Cook for 4 minutes.

Add the crumbled tofu, nutritional yeast, 2 tbsp water and the soy sauce to the pan. Stir well and cook for another 3 minutes, stirring frequently. Remove from the heat and stir in the baby spinach until it has wilted. Add the chopped herbs, salt and pepper to taste. Serve the tofu with the alfalfa sprouts and toast.

Feed Me
QUICKLY

This Japanese-inspired dish is easy to make, low in fat and packed with sweet flavour. The scored flesh tastes delicious once it has been grilled in the oven with the miso glaze. It has the perfect combination of sweet and salty flavours and can be served as a main if you are in the mood for something a bit lighter.

Miso-Glazed AUBERGINE

SERVES 2

2 aubergines, halved
    lengthways
2 tbsp light olive oil
2 tbsp white miso
2 tbsp mirin
2 tbsp caster sugar
2 spring onions, finely sliced
    on the diagonal
1 tbsp toasted sesame seeds
Sea salt

Preheat the oven to 200°C (180°C fan, gas 6). Using a small sharp knife, score the flesh of each aubergine half. Brush the scored side with olive oil and sprinkle with a little salt. Cook on the top shelf of the oven for 25 minutes.

Meanwhile, make a miso glaze. Put the miso, mirin and sugar in a small bowl and mix until smooth. Remove the aubergines from the oven and leave to cool for 2 minutes. Pour off any excess liquid.

Preheat the grill to medium-high. Spoon the miso mixture over each aubergine half and spread evenly to the edges. Put the aubergines under the grill for 5-7 minutes or until brown and caramelised. Serve the aubergines sprinkled with spring onions and sesame seeds.

Although salads are not necessarily my favourite choice when it comes to lunch or dinner I felt it necessary to include a couple for all those salad lovers out there! The cooked beetroot in this one is succulent, and complemented nicely by the simple dressing and crunchy nuts. As salads go it really is a favourite of mine, ideal if you're in the mood for something light and healthy.

Heritage Beetroot SALAD

SERVES 2

1 candy beetroot
1 golden beetroot
2 red beetroots
80g green beans
1 tbsp aged balsamic vinegar
2 tbsp extra virgin olive oil
Leaves from 2 thyme sprigs
60g mix of rocket, spinach
    and watercress leaves
30g toasted hazelnuts,
    roughly chopped
Sea salt and freshly ground
    black pepper

For the dressing:
1 tbsp red wine vinegar
1 tsp Dijon mustard
A pinch of sugar
3 tbsp extra virgin olive oil

Preheat the oven to 220°C (200°C fan, gas 7). Wrap each beetroot in foil. Put onto a baking tray and cook in the oven for 1½–2 hours until cooked through and soft when pressed. Meanwhile, cook the green beans in a steamer over boiling water for 5 minutes, then refresh under cold water. Leave to one side.

Put the balsamic vinegar, oil and thyme leaves in a bowl and whisk together until combined. Leave to one side.

Peel the red beetroot and cut it into thick wedges while it is still warm. Add it to the bowl with the balsamic to marinade.

Peel the candy and golden beetroots, and slice thickly. Put these in a large mixing bowl with the salad leaves, green beans and dressing. Serve the salad topped with the marinated beetroot and sprinkled with hazelnuts.

A nother easy meal when you've been having a bit of a comfort-eating spell . . . The only issue with salads is that sometimes you'll eat one and you'll still feel empty, which leaves you craving more food. Adding sweet potato to your salad it makes it a lot more filling, so you're far less likely to reach for the junk food!

Quinoa, Sweet Potato & Kale SALAD

SERVES 2

250g pack cooked red and
   white quinoa
400g sweet potatoes, cut into
   1cm slices
2 tbsp extra virgin olive oil
½ tsp ground cumin
80g nuts, such as almonds,
   pecan nuts and hazelnuts
100g kale, cut into bite-sized
   pieces
Sea salt and freshly ground
   black pepper

For the dressing:
4 tbsp extra virgin olive oil
Juice of 1 lemon
1 tbsp sherry vinegar
1 tsp Dijon mustard
1 tsp agave syrup
½ garlic clove, crushed

Preheat the oven to 200˚C (180˚C fan, gas 6) and line a baking tray with greaseproof paper.

Put the sweet potatoes on the prepared baking tray and add the oil, cumin, and salt and pepper. Mix well with your hands and then spread out the slices in a single layer. Cook on the top shelf of the oven for 20 minutes. Turn each slice over and return to the oven for a further 15 minutes.

Place the nuts onto a small oven tray and bake for 5–7 minutes or until golden brown. Leave to cool, then chop them roughly.

Put the kale in a mixing bowl. To make the dressing, put all the ingredients in a screwtop jar and add a little salt and pepper. Shake well to combine. Pour two-thirds of the dressing over the kale, then massage the kale with your hands for 2 minutes. This helps to soften the kale a little.

Mix in the quinoa and sweet potato and place onto serving plates. Serve with the remaining dressing and sprinkled with the toasted nuts.

Soups are so easy to make, but it's great to have a few different options so I wanted to put all my favourites into this book. This one is a guilt-free alternative to chicken noodle soup – the kind of thing you want if it's a cold night and you're tucked up with a cosy blanket. Make this for a friend who isn't feeling too great, and they'll thank you – it's delightful.

TOFU 'Chicken' NOODLE SOUP

SERVES 1

100g firm tofu, cut into
   2 slices
1 tbsp liquid aminos
1 tsp sesame oil, plus extra
   to drizzle
50g dried rice noodles
1 tbsp vegetable oil
1 vegetable stock cube
1 garlic clove, crushed
1cm piece of fresh root ginger,
   peeled and finely grated
1 tsp soy sauce
3 baby corn, halved
3 baby chestnut mushrooms,
   halved
6 mangetouts
1 small handful of Asian leafy
   greens, such as pak choi
   or Chinese cabbage
1 small handful of
   beansprouts
1 red chilli, deseeded and
   thinly sliced
2 tbsp each coriander
   and mint leaves

Put the tofu into a shallow bowl and pour over the aminos and sesame oil. Leave to marinate for 15 minutes, turning the tofu over once.

Put the rice noodles in a small heatproof bowl and cover with boiling water. Leave for 2–3 minutes until softened. Drain the noodles in a colander and refresh under cold water until cool. Drain and put into a serving bowl. Leave to one side.

Heat the vegetable oil in a small non-stick frying pan over a high heat. Remove the tofu from the marinade and lightly dry with kitchen paper. Put the tofu in the pan and cook for 2–3 minutes on each side until golden. Remove from heat and pour over the remaining marinade.

Put 400ml water into a small saucepan over a high heat. Crumble in the stock cube and add the garlic, ginger and soy sauce. Bring to the boil and add the baby corn, then cook for 2 minutes.

Add the mushrooms and mangetouts, and cook for 2 minutes more. Add the Asian greens and beansprouts, then remove from the heat. Transfer to the bowl with the noodles and top with the tofu slices, red chilli and herb leaves, then drizzle over the sesame oil and serve.

Healthy and hearty, this soup is ideal if you've been a bit under the weather, or you simply feel like being good to yourself. Soup is so comforting, I try to make a big batch when I can as it's not too heavy and keeps so well. The variety of veggies means this is brimming with flavour, as well as being low cal and totally guilt-free.

Pearl Barley & Vegetable SOUP

SERVES 4

1 tbsp olive oil

1 onion, finely diced

1 carrot, cut into small dice

2 garlic cloves, finely chopped

2 celery sticks, diced

1 tbsp thyme leaves

80g pearl barley

1 litre vegetable stock

100g broccoli florets,
  finely sliced

1 tomato, diced

1 handful of baby spinach
  leaves, chopped

Sea salt and freshly ground
  black pepper

For the basil pesto:

2 tbsp pine nuts

2 large handfuls of basil
  leaves

2 tbsp vegan Parmesan
  cheese, grated

Juice of ½ lemon

80ml extra virgin olive oil,
  plus extra to drizzle

Heat the oil in a large non-stick saucepan over a medium heat, then add the onion and cook for 5 minutes or until softened and translucent. Add the carrot, garlic and celery, and cook for 5 minutes.

Add the thyme leaves to the pan followed by the pearl barley and vegetable stock. Bring to the boil then reduce the heat and simmer for 20 minutes.

Meanwhile, make the pesto. Put the pine nuts in a small pan over a medium heat and cook for 1–2 minutes or until golden, shaking the pan frequently. Remove from the pan. Put the basil leaves in a blender or food processor and add the pine nuts, Parmesan, lemon juice and oil, then add a little salt and pepper. Blend until smooth, then leave to one side.

Add the broccoli and tomato to the pan and cook for 5 minutes. Season with salt and pepper to taste.

When you are ready to serve, stir in the spinach. Serve the soup with the pesto on top and drizzled with extra virgin olive oil.

The warm flavours in this soup go well together and it's super quick to prepare. I've included an olive tapenade as well here, which adds a great salty bite to the smoothness of the soup. It just provides something a bit different and is perfect to spread on any bread you want to use for dipping.

Roasted Red Pepper & Tomato SOUP

SERVES 4

5 red peppers, stalks removed, halved and deseeded

1kg ripe vine tomatoes, halved and cores removed

8 large garlic cloves, unpeeled

3 tbsp extra virgin olive oil

1 tbsp dried oregano

700ml vegetable stock

1 tsp paprika

2 tbsp tomato purée

4 baguette slices, toasted

Sea salt and freshly ground black pepper

For the black olive tapenade:

170g pitted black olives

2 small garlic cloves, crushed

2 tbsp baby capers

2 tbsp flat-leaf parsley leaves, roughly chopped

40ml extra virgin olive oil

Preheat the oven to 200°C (180°C fan, gas 6) and line two baking trays with greaseproof paper. Divide the peppers and tomatoes between the prepared baking trays. Add 4 garlic cloves to each tray. Drizzle with the oil and sprinkle with oregano, salt and pepper. Cook in the oven for 30 minutes.

Leave the trays to cool for a few minutes, then pick out the garlic cloves and remove their skins. Return the garlic, and tip the contents of both trays into a large saucepan. Pour over the vegetable stock and add the paprika and tomato purée. Bring to the boil, then reduce the heat to a simmer and cook for 15 minutes. Remove from the heat.

Meanwhile, make the tapenade. Put the olives into a small food processor and add the garlic, capers, parsley and oil. Season with a little salt and pepper – be careful not to add too much salt, because the olives will be quite salty already. Pulse the mixture until it comes together to form a rough paste. Spread this tapenade over the toasted baguette.

Ladle the soup mixture into a blender or food processor and blend until smooth. Serve the soup with the slices of olive toast.

Another one of my go-tos – the choice of veg in this makes it feel that bit more substantial. Cook up of an evening, or this would also work brilliantly as a starter if you're having friends round for dinner.

Butternut Squash & Sweet Potato SOUP —

SERVES 4

3 tbsp vegan butter
2 large garlic cloves,
 finely chopped
500g butternut squash, diced
500g sweet potato, diced
1 tbsp thyme leaves
1 litre vegetable stock
200ml coconut cream
Sea salt and freshly ground
 black pepper

For the topping:
50g pumpkin seeds
1 tsp liquid aminos

Melt the butter in a large saucepan over a medium heat. When hot, add the garlic and cook for 1 minute. Add the squash, sweet potato and thyme leaves, then stir well and cook for 5 minutes.

Pour the vegetable stock into the saucepan, bring to the boil, then reduce the heat to a simmer. Cover and cook gently for 10 minutes. Remove the lid and simmer for another 10 minutes.

Meanwhile, put the pumpkin seeds for the topping in a small frying pan over a medium-high heat and toast them for 2–3 minutes until they begin to pop. Remove from heat and pour the aminos over the pumpkin seeds, then stir well and leave to cool.

Pour 4 tbsp of the coconut cream into a bowl. Loosen with a little water until it's the consistency of double cream. Pour the remaining coconut cream into the saucepan and cook for 5 minutes. Season the soup with salt and pepper. Ladle the mixture into a blender or food processor and blend until smooth.

Serve the soup with 1 tbsp coconut cream drizzled over each bowl and a sprinkle of toasted pumpkin seeds on top.

*P*ea and mint is one of my absolute favourite soups so this one had to be included. Served with warm bread, this is a filling and delicious meal, perfect for an evening tucked up on the sofa. This is another soup I tend to make in big batches as you can keep them in the fridge or even freeze them – they last for ages. Great if you know you have a busy week ahead!

Pea & Mint SOUP

SERVES 4

1 tbsp olive oil

2 tbsp vegan butter

2 leeks, finely sliced

2 garlic cloves, finely chopped

600g potatoes, finely chopped

1.2 litres vegetable stock

600g frozen peas, thawed

A handful of mint leaves

Extra virgin olive oil, to drizzle

Sea salt and freshly ground
   black pepper

Croutons and pea shoots,
   to garnish

Heat the oil and butter in a large saucepan over a medium heat. Add the leeks and garlic, and cook for 5–7 minutes until softened.

Add the potatoes and vegetable stock, and cook for 15 minutes or until the potatoes are done. Save a handful of peas for the garnish, then add the remaining peas and the mint to the pan, and cook for a further 5 minutes. Season the soup with salt and pepper.

Blend until smooth in a blender or food processor. Serve drizzled with olive oil and sprinkled with croutons, the reserved peas and the pea shoots.

The first of a few Asian-inspired dishes, miso soup usually contains fish sauce but is very easy to make vegan friendly (plus it tastes the same as the non-vegan kind – so really the fish is just unnecessary). The brown rice and cavolo nero give this one more substance, and together they make a hearty, soul-warming dish.

MISO SOUP WITH
Brown Rice & Cavolo Nero

SERVES 1

100g cooked brown rice
  (you will need about 50g
  uncooked rice to make
  100g cooked rice – for
  instructions on cooking rice
  see page 59)
1 tbsp miso paste
1 tsp liquid aminos
1 tsp mirin
1 handful of cavolo nero,
  roughly chopped
80g firm tofu, cubed
1 tsp dried wakame seaweed

For the garnish:
1 spring onion, finely sliced
1 tbsp crispy onion
1 tsp roasted sesame seeds

Put 350ml water into a saucepan and bring to the boil. Stir in the miso paste, aminos and mirin. Add the cavolo nero, rice and tofu and bring the soup back to the boil, then reduce the heat to a simmer. Cook for 2–3 minutes or until the cavolo nero is tender.

Stir in the wakame, then serve the soup garnished with spring onion, crispy onion and sesame seeds.

Stir-fries are such a great quick week-night meal – if you've had a long day and you want to be able to whizz something up then this is the one for you. Soba noodles are great as they're made from buckwheat, which contains heaps of protein. I love a Chinese takeaway but they're really not that good for you, so if you make a stir-fry at home you can benefit from a much healthier version of one of your favourite meals. Feel free to throw in some tofu or vegan Quorn if you're seeking extra protein.

Stir-Fried SOBA NOODLES

SERVES 2

200g soba noodles
2 tbsp groundnut oil
2 garlic cloves, finely chopped
2.5cm piece of fresh root
    ginger, peeled and cut
    into thin strips
½ long red chilli, deseeded
    and finely diced
6 baby corn, diagonally sliced
½ red pepper, deseeded
    and sliced
100g chestnut mushrooms
½ courgette, halved lengthways
    and diagonally sliced
2 pak choi, cut into 2.5cm pieces
3 spring onions, diagonally
    sliced
2 tbsp soy sauce
2 tbsp teriyaki sauce
1 tbsp sesame oil
1 handful of beansprouts
1 handful of coriander leaves,
    roughly chopped
Sliced spring onions and sliced
    red chilli, to garnish

Cook the soba noodles in boiling salted water according to the packet instructions, until al dente. When cooked, drain in a colander and refresh with cold water until cool. Leave to one side.

Heat the oil in a non-stick wok over a high heat. When hot, add the garlic, ginger and chilli. Stir-fry for 30 seconds, then add the baby corn and 3 tbsp water.

When the water has evaporated, add the pepper and mushrooms, then stir-fry for 3 minutes. Add the courgette, pak choi, noodles and spring onions along with 2 tbsp water, the soy sauce, teriyaki sauce and sesame oil. Stir-fry for 3–4 minutes until the noodles are hot and the sauce has thickened.

Remove from the heat and add the beansprouts and coriander. Give the wok a quick toss and serve the noodles in deep bowls, garnished with sliced spring onions and red chilli.

This is one of those 'picture perfect' meals that also tastes amazing! It has pretty much everything in it: tofu, veggies, rice and nuts with the satay sauce complementing all the elements perfectly. It's an all-rounder that is easy to throw together – just take care with the presentation and get your phone ready for sharing!

PEANUT TOFU *Buddha Bowl*

SERVES 2

180g sweet potato, cut into
    large dice
1 small red onion, cut into
    large dice
1 tbsp olive oil
70g brown rice
140g firm tofu, cut into
    large dice
1 tbsp liquid aminos
1 tbsp light olive oil
½ ripe avocado, pitted
¼ cucumber, sliced
1 handful of spinach
1 handful of alfalfa
1 tbsp toasted sesame seeds
2 tbsp roasted peanuts
Sea salt and freshly ground
    black pepper

For the satay sauce:
2 tbsp crunchy peanut butter
Juice from ½ lime
1 tbsp soy sauce
1 tsp extra virgin olive oil
1 tsp sesame oil
1 tsp agave syrup

Preheat the oven to 200°C (180°C fan, gas 6) and line a baking tray with greaseproof paper. Lay the sweet potato and onion on the prepared tray. Drizzle with olive oil and season with salt and pepper. Mix well with your hands, then cook in the oven for 30 minutes.

Meanwhile, rinse your rice then put it in a saucepan and add 2½ times the volume of water. Bring to the boil, then reduce the heat and simmer for 30 minutes or until tender, stirring once or twice. Drain in a colander and leave to one side to cool.

Put the tofu and aminos in a shallow bowl, mix well and leave to marinate for 15 minutes.

Put all the ingredients for the satay sauce in a bowl and stir well to combine. Leave to one side.

Heat the oil in a non-stick frying pan. Add the tofu and cook for 5 minutes, stirring frequently, then continue to cook until the tofu is golden brown on all sides. Scoop the flesh from the avocado using a tablespoon and slice it.

Prepare the bowls by putting the rice in first. Divide the roasted sweet potato between the bowls. Add the tofu, cucumber, spinach, alfalfa and avocado. Pour over the satay sauce and sprinkle with sesame seeds and peanuts to serve.

I never used to be a fan of pesto but when you become vegan you suddenly decide that you want to be able to eat anything and everything that you now 'aren't allowed' to eat. It's like being reborn and you can start all over again with new tastes and flavours. This pesto is delicious and creamy and if you can stop yourself eating it all, there should be enough for leftovers!

Spinach & Pesto PASTA

SERVES 2

180g cherry tomatoes, halved
2 tbsp extra virgin olive oil
1 tsp dried oregano
250g rigatoni pasta
A good pinch of grated
    nutmeg
Sea salt and freshly ground
    black pepper

For the spinach & pesto sauce:
30g pine nuts
150g baby spinach
30g basil leaves
1 garlic clove, crushed
80ml extra virgin olive oil
30g vegan Parmesan cheese,
    grated
2 tbsp single soya cream

Preheat the oven to 160°C (140°C fan, gas 3) and line a small baking tray with greaseproof paper. Lay the cherry tomatoes cut-side up on the prepared baking tray. Drizzle with the oil and sprinkle with oregano. Season with a little salt and pepper. Cook in the oven for 1¼ hours.

Meanwhile, to make the pesto sauce, put the pine nuts in a small pan over a medium heat and cook for 1–2 minutes until golden, shaking the pan frequently. Remove from the pan. Put the spinach, basil, garlic and oil into a blender or food processor. Add half the pine nuts and half the grated Parmesan cheese. Season with salt and pepper, and blend until smooth.

When the tomatoes are cooked, remove them from the oven and leave to cool. Cook the rigatoni in boiling salted water according to the packet instructions, until al dente. Drain in a colander.

Meanwhile, put the pesto in a large non-stick frying pan and bring to a simmer. Add the soya cream, salt and pepper, and stir well. Add the rigatoni to the pan with the sauce. Toss well to coat the pasta. Add half the cherry tomatoes to the sauce, stir well and serve in bowls topped with the remaining Parmesan, pine nuts and cherry tomatoes and the grated nutmeg.

A nyone who knows me will know about my mac and cheese obsession. I struggle to understand why you wouldn't like mac and cheese! Whenever I tried to switch to veganism previously this was the dish that would make me relapse. I just couldn't resist it. So I HAD to find a good recipe for mac and cheese – one that would actually taste similar to the original. Many of the recipes I tried use cashews, but I never felt they were successful at recreating the flavours and textures. Thankfully, this one is spot-on and the mushrooms add an extra texture and flavour that take it to the next level! For the vegan cheese I would use the Cheddar or Parmesan from Follow Your Heart – though Violife Parmesan and Sheese Cheddar are also really good with this.

Mushroomy MAC 'N' CHEESE

SERVES 6

500g dried macaroni
40g dried wild mushrooms
2 tbsp vegan butter
250g chestnut mushrooms
2 garlic cloves, finely chopped
1 tbsp thyme leaves
Sea salt and freshly ground
   black pepper

For the béchamel sauce:
50g vegan butter
3 tbsp plain flour
800ml almond milk
¼ tsp grated nutmeg
4 tbsp nutritional yeast
200g vegan Cheddar cheese,
   grated
50g vegan Parmesan cheese,
   finely grated

For the topping:
40g vegan Parmesan cheese,
   grated
2 tbsp finely chopped flat-leaf
   parsley leaves

Preheat the oven to 220˚C (200˚C fan, gas 7). Cook the macaroni in boiling, salted water according to the packet instructions, until al dente. Drain in a colander and refresh under cold water until cooled.

Put the dried mushrooms in a small heatproof bowl. Pour 150ml boiling water over them and leave them to rehydrate for 15 minutes. Drain the mushrooms from the liquid, reserving it for the béchamel sauce. Roughly chop the mushrooms.

Melt the butter in a non-stick frying pan over a high heat. When hot, add the wild mushrooms, chestnut mushrooms, garlic and thyme. Cook for 5–8 minutes until the mushrooms have browned well. Season with salt and pepper, and remove from the heat.

To make the béchamel sauce, put a large saucepan over a medium heat, then add the butter and stir until melted. Add the flour and cook for 1 minute, stirring constantly. Whisk in the milk, and continue to whisk until the sauce thickens, then lower the heat and add the remaining ingredients. Stir until the cheese has completely melted. Remove from the heat and season with salt and pepper.

Add the mushrooms and macaroni to the saucepan with the sauce and stir well until everything is evenly coated in the sauce. Transfer to a deep 25 × 30cm ovenproof dish.

Mix the topping ingredients together and sprinkle over the macaroni. Cook in the oven for 20–25 minutes or until the topping is golden brown and crunchy.

Feed Me
FEASTS

My favourite time! Where do I start? Pizza and I have had a longstanding, successful relationship and I wasn't about to put an end to that when I turned vegan. Nowadays there are some great vegan pizza places out there (which makes me so happy) but there's nothing like homemade pizza. You can get stuck in and add as many toppings as you want, there's really no holding back. I recommend using specific 'pizza cheese' from Veganic; Violife also does a good one. I like to add as many veggies as possible and (controversially to some) love to throw on pineapple. The choice is yours, let the kneading begin . . .

PIZZA *Time*

MAKES 2× 25CM PIZZAS

7g sachet active dried yeast

1 tsp caster sugar

1 tbsp extra virgin olive oil,
   plus extra for greasing

250g strong white bread flour,
   plus extra for dusting

½ tsp fine sea salt

For the pizza sauce:

120ml passata

2 tbsp tomato purée

1 garlic clove, crushed

1 tbsp extra virgin olive oil

Sea salt and freshly ground
   black pepper

For the topping:

250g vegan pizza cheese,
   grated

4 mushrooms, sliced

½ courgette, thinly sliced

8 artichoke hearts from a jar
   or can, cut into quarters

120g roasted red peppers,
   cut into strips

16 pitted Kalamata olives

Rocket leaves, to garnish

Put the yeast in a bowl and add 150ml warm water, the sugar and oil. Stir to mix then leave for 5–10 minutes to activate and become frothy. Put the flour and salt in a large bowl. Make a well in the centre and gradually pour in the yeast liquid, stirring as you go until the mixture forms a ball of dough.

Lightly flour the work surface and knead the dough for 5 minutes or until smooth. Lightly grease the bowl and put the dough inside. Cover the bowl with clingfilm and leave it in a warm place until the dough doubles in size.

Preheat the oven to 240°C (220°C fan, gas 9) and flour two baking trays. Make the pizza sauce by mixing all the ingredients together in a bowl. Season with salt and pepper.

When the dough has risen, knock it back and divide it into two balls. Roll each one to a 25cm circle and put onto the prepared baking trays.

Divide the pizza sauce between the two pizzas, leaving a 1cm rim around the edge. Sprinkle each one with a quarter of the cheese. Add the other toppings and sprinkle with the remaining cheese. Season each pizza with a little salt and pepper. Cook on the two top shelves of the oven for 12 minutes or until the cheese is bubbling and the dough is crusty. Serve cut into wedges and sprinkled with a few rocket leaves.

This dish has to be one of my favourites as I'm a huge pasta lover. It's creamy and delicious, the squash gives it a slight sweet kick and the béchamel sauce tastes just the same as the non-vegan kind. I was apprehensive about recreating lasagne as so many of the ingredients aren't vegan-friendly, but it turned out to be a huge success. You'll be happy (and maybe even surprised) to know that most lasagne sheets are actually vegan, which makes things a lot easier. I dare you to serve this to someone and see if they even notice it's vegan!

BUTTERNUT SQUASH
& Spinach Lasagne

SERVES 6

750g butternut squash,
    cut into ½ cm slices

3 portobello mushrooms,
    cut into 1cm slices

4 tbsp extra virgin olive oil

1 tbsp thyme leaves

2 garlic cloves, finely chopped

80g vegan butter

70g plain flour

800ml soya milk

½ tsp grated nutmeg

2 tbsp nutritional yeast

150g vegan Cheddar cheese,
    grated

200g artichoke hearts from
    a jar or can, sliced

60g vegan Parmesan cheese,
    finely grated

250g vegan fresh lasagne
    sheets

75g baby spinach leaves

Salt and freshly ground
    black pepper

Preheat the oven to 200°C (180°C fan, gas 6). Line three baking trays with greaseproof paper. Divide the butternut squash slices between two baking trays in a single layer. Drizzle 1 tbsp of the olive oil over each tray and season generously with salt and pepper. Cook in the oven for 25 minutes.

Lay the mushrooms on the remaining tray. Drizzle with 2 tbsp oil. Sprinkle with thyme and garlic, and season with salt and pepper. Cook in the oven for 20 minutes.

Meanwhile, make a cheese sauce. Melt the butter in a saucepan over a medium heat. Add the flour and cook for 1 minute, stirring. Whisk in the milk until the sauce begins to thicken slightly. Stir in the nutmeg, nutritional yeast, Cheddar cheese and artichoke hearts. Add half the Parmesan cheese and stir until melted. Season with salt and pepper, and remove from heat.

Spread a thin layer of the sauce on the base of a deep 25 × 30cm baking dish to prevent the pasta sticking to the base. Lay a quarter of the lasagne sheets over the top and ladle a quarter of the sauce over. Spread out evenly and lay the butternut squash from one tray over the sauce.

Add another layer of pasta and a quarter of the sauce. Spread out evenly, then add the cooked mushrooms in a single layer. Add another layer of pasta, followed by a quarter of the sauce. Lay the remaining butternut squash over the sauce and spread the baby spinach leaves over the top.

Lastly, add the remaining lasagne sheets. Top with the remaining sauce and sprinkle with the remaining Parmesan. Cook in the centre of the oven for 40 minutes, then serve.

They really are as good as they look in the picture – I would go as far as saying they are my favourite burgers ever! A lot of people ask 'but where do you get your protein?' and it's honestly not that hard. So many foods, particularly grains and pulses, contain proteins. These burgers are made mainly out of lentils and chickpeas, and the smoked hickory gives them that 'meaty' flavour. They're really easy to make, though make sure you do allow the time for them to firm up in the fridge – if you're rushing, pop them in the freezer for half an hour. I use a slice of Sheese Cheddar when I put them in the oven – it melts just right and tastes spot-on.

ULTIMATE *Cheeseburger*

MAKES 4

4 tbsp olive oil
1 onion, finely diced
2 garlic cloves, finely chopped
1 red pepper, deseeded and
   diced
1 tsp ground cumin
1 tsp salt
2 tsp hickory liquid smoke
400g can chickpeas, drained
   and rinsed
40g rolled oats
250g cooked Puy lentils from
   a can or pack, drained
50g plain flour
4 slices vegan Cheddar cheese
Freshly ground black pepper

To serve:
4 wholemeal burger buns,
   halved and toasted
Vegan mayonnaise
8 Little Gem lettuce leaves
Ketchup
2 dill pickles, sliced thickly
American mustard
French fries

Heat 2 tbsp of the oil in a non-stick frying pan over a high heat. Add the onion and cook for 3–4 minutes or until softened and translucent. Add the garlic and red pepper, and cook for 4 minutes. Stir in the cumin and salt, cook for 1 minute and then remove from heat. Leave to cool.

Put the onion mixture into a food processor, followed by the liquid smoke and chickpeas. Pulse until the mixture combines but is not smooth – you want to retain some texture. Transfer this mixture to a large bowl.

Put the rolled oats into the cleaned food processor and blend until they resemble a coarse flour. Add this to the bowl followed by the cooked lentils. Mix well and season with black pepper. Divide the mixture into four equal burgers and transfer to the fridge for 2–3 hours until firm.

Preheat the oven to 200°C (180°C fan, gas 6). Sprinkle the flour over the burgers on both sides. Dust off any excess flour.

Heat the remaining oil in a non-stick frying pan over a high heat. Add the burgers and cook for 2–3 minutes on each side until browned. Transfer to a baking tray and cook in the oven for 5 minutes. Remove from the oven, add a slice of cheese to each burger and return it to the oven for 2–3 minutes until the cheese has melted.

Spread each bun with some mayonnaise. Put 2 lettuce leaves on the bottom half of each bun. Top with the burger, ketchup, dill pickles, more mayo and the mustard. Serve with hot, crispy fries.

Another brilliant burger recipe that is really yummy! Sweet potatoes are involved in a lot of my meals because they're healthy and delicious, and they go with pretty much everything. This patty is both sweet and savoury and gluten free (if you go for a gluten-free bun). It's really easy to make and goes perfectly with my Oreo milkshake (see page 116) if you're having one of those slouchy days where you just want to be sickeningly full. We all have them.

Sweet Potato & Black Bean
BURGERS

MAKES 2

2 small sweet potatoes,
   unpeeled
50g walnuts
400g can black beans,
   drained and rinsed
1 tsp sweet smoked paprika
½ tsp garlic powder
½ tsp Italian herbs
Salt and freshly ground
   black pepper

For the fennel slaw:
120g fennel, finely shredded
2 tbsp vegan mayonnaise
1 tsp white wine vinegar
1 tbsp dill leaves, finely
   chopped

To serve:
½ ripe avocado, pitted
2 wholemeal burger buns,
   halved and toasted
1 handful of spinach

Preheat the oven to 180°C (160°C fan, gas 4). Prick the sweet potatoes with a fork and put them on a small baking tray. Cook on the top shelf of the oven for 40 minutes or until soft and cooked through.

Meanwhile, put the walnuts in a small pan and toast them over a medium-high heat for 1–2 minutes or until evenly toasted, shaking the pan frequently. Tip out of the pan onto a plate. Put half the black beans into a food processor followed by the walnuts, and blend until smooth. Tip this mixture into a mixing bowl, along with the remaining black beans. Add the paprika, garlic powder and Italian herbs, and season with salt and pepper.

Remove the cooked sweet potatoes from the oven and leave them until cool enough to handle. Cut them in half and scoop out the flesh into a bowl, then mash it lightly. Mix this with the black bean mixture. Divide into two portions and flatten into burgers. Leave to set in the fridge for 1 hour.

Preheat the oven to 200°C (180°C fan, gas 6) and line a small baking tray with greaseproof paper. Put the burgers onto the prepared baking tray and bake for 35 minutes.

While the burgers are cooking, make the fennel slaw by mixing all the ingredients together. To serve, scoop the flesh from the avocado using a tablespoon and slice it. Put a burger on the bottom half of each bun. Top with fennel slaw, avocado and spinach and finish with the top half of the bun.

This one is a go-to in my house and proves a protein-packed meal for those friends (or boyfriends) who are particularly concerned about their protein intake. Protein is something that gets mentioned a lot when going vegan, but there are so many options and beans are one of the many plant-based foods that are packed with protein. This goes great with nachos (see page 150) and rice. I tend to make a big batch and keep it in the fridge to have for lunch when I'm feeling lazy.

BLACK BEAN *Chilli*

SERVES 4

2 tbsp olive oil

1 tbsp cumin seeds

1 onion, cut into 1cm dice

1 green jalapeño chilli,
    finely chopped

3 garlic cloves, finely chopped

1 red pepper, deseeded and
    cut into 1cm dice

1 yellow pepper, deseeded
    and cut into 1cm dice

1 tbsp paprika

1 tsp dried oregano

2 × 400g cans black beans,
    drained and rinsed

400g can red kidney beans,
    drained and rinsed

400g can chopped tomatoes

1 tbsp apple cider vinegar

Sea salt and freshly ground
    black pepper

Coriander leaves and sliced
    pickled jalapeño chillies,
    to garnish

Corn chips, to serve

For the pickled red onion:
1 red onion, finely sliced
Juice of 1 lime

Put a large sauté pan over a high heat. When the pan is hot, add the oil and cumin seeds. Once the seeds begin to sizzle, add the onion and cook for 3–4 minutes, until softened, stirring well. Add the chilli and garlic, stir well and cook for 2 minutes more. Stir in the peppers and cook for 3–4 minutes until softened, then stir in the paprika and oregano.

Cook for 1 minute, then add the beans. Pour in the canned tomatoes, then fill the can with water and swish it around to get all the remaining bits of tomato from the can; pour this into the pan along with the cider vinegar. Stir well and season with salt and pepper. Bring the chilli to the boil, then reduce the heat and simmer for 15 minutes.

Meanwhile, to make the pickled onion, put the onion in a heatproof bowl and cover with boiling water. Leave for 5 minutes. Drain off the water and squeeze over the lime, then add a pinch of salt. Mix well and leave for 15 minutes. It will slowly start to turn an intense pink.

Serve the chilli in bowls with the pickled onion and garnished with coriander and pickled jalapeño chillies. Serve with lots of corn chips alongside to dip.

*F*ajitas are another dish that I grew up enjoying, though as I was vegetarian from so young I always ate them with Quorn chicken. Quorn (make sure it's the vegan version) works so well with anything that would originally be chicken based that meat-eating friends of mine have said the taste is very similar. The best fun with this recipe is creating your own fajita and choosing how fully-loaded you want to make it!

FAJITAS *with Corn Salsa*

SERVES 4

2 tbsp light olive oil

2 garlic cloves, finely chopped

1 green jalapeño chilli,
    deseeded and finely chopped

½ red pepper, deseeded and
    thickly sliced

½ yellow pepper, deseeded
    and thickly sliced

½ green pepper, deseeded
    and thickly sliced

280g pack Quorn vegan pieces,
    thawed

Fajita spice blend

6–8 tortillas

2 tbsp A1 steak sauce

For the corn salsa:

2 corn cobs, trimmed

1 large ripe tomato, finely
    chopped

2 spring onions, finely sliced

4 slices of pickled jalapeño
    chilli, finely chopped

1 tbsp finely chopped
    coriander leaves

Juice of 1 lime

1 tbsp extra virgin olive oil

Sea salt and freshly ground
    black pepper

To make the corn salsa, put the corn cobs in a large saucepan of boiling water and boil for 25 minutes or until the kernels are golden and tender. Drain.

Heat a large non-stick frying pan over a high heat. When hot, add the corn cobs and cook for 3–4 minutes on each side until slightly charred. As soon as one side is charred, turn it over a little to char on all sides.

Remove from the pan and leave to cool for a few minutes, then run a sharp knife down each side of the cob to remove the kernels. Put the charred corn kernels in a bowl and add the tomato, spring onions, chilli, coriander, lime juice and oil. Season with salt and pepper. Stir well and leave to one side.

Preheat the oven to 170°C (150°C fan, gas 3). Heat a non stick sauté pan over a high heat. Add the oil, garlic, chilli and peppers, and cook for 3–4 minutes until softened. Next, put in the Quorn pieces and fajita spices, then cook for 1–2 minutes, stirring occasionally. Add 80ml water and cook for 10 minutes, stirring frequently.

Meanwhile, wrap the tortillas in foil and put them on a baking tray. Warm through in the oven for 5 minutes.

When the fajita mix is ready, transfer it into a serving bowl. Put the corn salsa into another bowl and put the warmed tortillas on a plate and the A1 sauce in a bowl on the table, and let everyone help themselves.

*P*erfect for on-the-go or for a healthy, yet filling, lunch. There's a bit of everything in here, and the black beans add a nice amount of protein. The kale gives it a delicious crunch and is full of nutrients!

Sweet Potato & Kale BURRITOS

SERVES 4

600g sweet potatoes, cut into
    long, thick wedges
2 tbsp olive oil
¼ tsp paprika
4 large tortillas
1 avocado, halved and pitted
Sea salt and freshly ground
    black pepper

For the pickled cabbage:
120g red cabbage, finely shredded
1 tbsp red wine vinegar
60g can corn kernels, drained

For the Mexican rice:
1 tbsp olive oil
½ onion, finely chopped
1 garlic clove, finely chopped
1 tsp ground cumin
1 tsp paprika
250g tomatoes, diced
250g cooked brown basmati rice
    (you will need about 125g
    uncooked rice – for instructions
    on cooking rice see page 59)
400g can black beans, drained
    and rinsed
80g soya cheese, grated

For the kale:
2 tbsp vegan butter
120g kale

Preheat the oven to 200˚C (180˚C fan, gas 6) and line a baking tray with greaseproof paper. Put the sweet potatoes on the prepared baking tray. Drizzle over the oil and sprinkle with paprika, salt and pepper. Mix well. Cook in the oven for 25–30 minutes until golden and tender.

Put the cabbage in a small bowl, add a pinch of salt and the red wine vinegar. Stir well, then add in the corn and put into the fridge until needed.

Heat the oil in a large non-stick frying pan. Add the onion and cook for 5 minutes or until softened and translucent. Tip in the garlic and cook for 2 minutes, then add the cumin and paprika, and cook for 1 minute. Add the tomatoes and 2 tbsp water. Bring to the boil, then reduce the heat and simmer for 5 minutes. Add the rice and black beans, and cook for a further 5 minutes or until the rice has heated through. Add the cheese and season with salt and pepper. Stir well until the cheese begins to melt, then remove from the heat.

To prepare the kale, melt the butter in a medium saucepan, add the kale and a splash of water, and cook until just wilted. Season with a little salt and pepper.

Heat the tortillas in the oven for 30 seconds. Scoop the flesh from the avocado using a tablespoon and cut into 8 wedges. Put a quarter of the rice in the centre of each tortilla. Add a large spoonful of kale, a handful of pickled cabbage, 3 wedges of sweet potato and 2 wedges of avocado. Tuck each side of the tortilla inwards and roll the tortilla tightly over the filling. Repeat with the remaining tortillas to make 4 neat burritos. Cut each one in half to serve.

A few years back I lived for two months in New York, where I became addicted to tacos. Although I still ate dairy products then, the options were pretty limited – I'd have really struggled to find a vegan option! So now I've created these tacos, which have a bit of everything, with loads of different flavours and textures. For this recipe I used the ready-marinated tofu from Cauldron, but if you prefer to marinate your tofu yourself, then be my guest. Using the pre-prepared tofu just makes everything that little bit quicker and easier to pull together, especially for you first-time vegans out there.

Smoky Chipotle TOFU TACOS

MAKES 6

2 tbsp olive oil

1 onion, finely chopped

200g mini portobello
mushrooms, diced

1 tsp sea salt

2 garlic cloves, finely chopped

160g pack marinated tofu pieces

250g tomatoes, diced

1 handful of coriander leaves,
roughly chopped

1½ tbsp chipotle in adobo

½ tsp hickory liquid smoke

6 hard corn taco shells

150g iceberg lettuce,
finely shredded

50g red cabbage, finely shredded

100g vegan cheese, grated

2 tomatoes, diced

Pickled red onion (see page 74)

For the guacamole:

2 ripe avocados, halved
and pitted

Juice of 1 lime

1 tsp white miso paste

2 tbsp soya yogurt

2 tbsp coriander leaves,
finely chopped

Sea salt and freshly ground
black pepper

To make the guacamole, scoop the flesh from the avocados into a small bowl using a tablespoon. Add the lime juice and mash together. Add the miso, yogurt and coriander, and season with a little salt and pepper. Mix well, then cover with clingfilm and keep in the fridge until needed.

Preheat the oven to 200°C (180°C fan, gas 6). Heat the oil in a large frying pan over a high heat. Add the onion and cook for 3–4 minutes or until softened. Next, put in the mushrooms, salt and garlic, and cook for 5 minutes or until the mushrooms are beginning to brown.

Add the tofu, tomatoes, chopped coriander and 2 tbsp water, then allow to simmer for 5 minutes. Add the chipotle and liquid smoke, and season with pepper.

Heat the tacos in the oven for 3–4 minutes until heated through. Meanwhile, mix the lettuce and red cabbage together.

Fill the tacos with the tofu mix, then top with the grated cheese, lettuce and cabbage, the guacamole, tomatoes and pickled red onion. Serve.

Risotto is really easy to make vegan, especially with butter and cheese alternatives being so great these days (see the Store Cupboard for my favourites). For anyone wondering if a vegan version lacks in flavour, it couldn't be more like what you're used to (obviously this one is more delicious).

Mushroom RISOTTO

SERVES 4

50g dried porcini mushrooms
1 litre vegetable stock
2 tbsp olive oil
1 small onion, finely chopped
2 garlic cloves, finely chopped
1 tbsp thyme leaves
150g chestnut mushrooms,
    thickly sliced
150g wild mushrooms
350g risotto rice, such
    as Arborio
200ml vegan white wine
20g vegan butter
2 tbsp finely chopped flat-leaf
    parsley leaves
30g vegan Parmesan cheese,
    finely grated
Sea salt and freshly ground
    black pepper

Put the dried porcini mushrooms in a bowl and pour over 200ml boiling water. Leave to rehydrate for 10 minutes. Strain the mushrooms over a bowl and reserve the liquid. Chop the mushrooms roughly. Pour the mushroom liquid into a saucepan and add the vegetable stock. Bring to the boil then, reduce the heat to a low simmer.

Heat the oil in a saucepan over a medium heat. Add the onion and cook for 5 minutes or until softened and translucent, then add the garlic and thyme and cook for 2 minutes. Add the porcini mushrooms and the chestnut mushrooms, then season with salt and pepper. Cook for 5 minutes, then stir in the wild mushrooms and rice. Stir well to let the grains of rice toast lightly in the pan for 1 minute.

Pour in the wine, then stir and let it bubble until most of it has completely evaporated. Add a quarter of the hot stock and stir often until the liquid has absorbed. Repeat this process twice more, making sure to stir until the liquid is absorbed. The mixture should now be creamy and almost cooked. Gradually add the last amount of stock, stirring as before. Remove from the heat. Season to taste and stir in the butter and parsley. Serve sprinkled with Parmesan cheese.

This has to be one of my favourite dishes in the book. I've always loved Italian food, especially creamy pastas, but when I turned vegan I limited myself to toppings like tomato sauce or oil and garlic. Soya cream and vegan cheese changed all that! The smokiness of the tofu and the vegan bacon give it that 'meaty' texture and taste, and the cream sauce is addictive! Sometimes I add in some peas, and it goes really well with a side salad or garlic bread.

LINGUINE *Carbonara*

SERVES 1

100g dried linguine

2 tbsp vegan butter

2 rashers vegan bacon,
   thickly sliced

50g smoked tofu, diced

1 small garlic clove,
   finely chopped

175ml soya cream

3 tbsp soya milk

A pinch of ground turmeric

20g Parmesan cheese,
   finely grated

1 tbsp finely chopped flat-leaf
   parsley leaves

Sea salt and freshly ground
   black pepper

Cook the linguine in a large pan of boiling salted water according to the packet instructions, until al dente. Drain in a colander and refresh with cold water until cool. Leave to one side.

Heat the butter in a non-stick frying pan over a medium heat. Add the bacon and tofu, and cook for 4–5 minutes or until they start to become crispy. Add the garlic and cook for another 2 minutes. Pour in the cream, milk, turmeric and half the Parmesan cheese. Reduce the heat to a gentle simmer and stir well.

Add the cooked pasta and cook for 2–3 minutes until heated through and well incorporated. Add the parsley and season with salt and pepper. Mix well and serve sprinkled with the remaining Parmesan and a little more black pepper.

This is another one of my top ten recipes; I go through phases of having it every other night! Even your more carnivorous friends won't realise this is vegan and it's PERFECT if you're cooking dinner for friends and family. Easy to make, the sauce is rich with flavour and it's full of chunky veg. Just the smell of the sauce gets me going, especially once the red wine goes in . . . Enjoy with some delicious, cruelty-free garlic bread.

Spaghetti BOLOGNESE

SERVES 6

20g dried wild mushrooms

2 tbsp olive oil

1 onion, finely chopped

2 carrots, finely chopped

3 celery sticks, finely chopped

2 garlic cloves, finely chopped

120g chestnut mushrooms, sliced

2 tbsp sundried tomato paste

½ tsp hot smoked paprika

250ml vegan red wine

700g passata

400g can chopped tomatoes

200ml vegetable stock

1 tbsp dried oregano

2 rosemary sprigs, leaves
    finely chopped

3 tbsp nutritional yeast

80g savoury soya protein mince (TVP)

500g spaghetti

50g vegan Parmesan cheese, grated

Sea salt and freshly ground
    black pepper

Basil leaves, to garnish

For the cheese and garlic bread:

6 tbsp vegan butter

3 large garlic cloves, crushed

60g vegan Parmesan cheese,
    finely grated

1 tbsp finely chopped flat-leaf
    parsley leaves

12 slices ciabatta bread

Put the dried wild mushrooms in a bowl and pour over 200ml boiling water. Leave to rehydrate for 10 minutes, then strain over a bowl and reserve the soaking liquid.

Heat the oil in a large non-stick saucepan over a medium heat. Add the onion and carrots, and cook for 5 minutes, until the onion is softened and translucent, then add the celery and garlic. Cook for 5 minutes, then add the chestnut mushrooms to the pan and cook for 2–3 minutes until softened. Roughly chop the soaked wild mushrooms and add them to the pan, followed by the sundried tomato paste and paprika. Stir and cook for 2 minutes.

Add the red wine and cook until the sauce reduces by half. Pour in the passata, tomatoes, reserved mushroom liquid and the stock. Add the oregano, rosemary and yeast. Season with salt and pepper, then return to a gentle simmer and cook for 15 minutes.

Meanwhile, preheat the oven to 180˚C (160˚C fan, gas 4). To make the cheese and garlic bread, put the butter in a small bowl and add the garlic, cheese and parsley. Season with salt and pepper and mix well. Spread this mixture onto the ciabatta slices and put onto a baking tray. Cook on the top shelf of the oven for 10 minutes. While the bread is cooking, preheat the grill and cook the spaghetti.

Boil the spaghetti in boiling salted water according to the packet instructions, until al dente. Drain in a colander.

Put the ciabatta under the grill for 2–3 minutes until golden on top. Add the soya mince to the sauce, stir and cook for 3 minutes. Serve the Bolognese with the spaghetti, topped with Parmesan and garnished with basil, with the cheese and garlic bread alongside.

*W*ell . . . Not quite. But definitely similar! Just minus the meat . . . I know how hard the vegan transition can be at times, and how you can feel like you're missing out on variety. These are obviously inspired by spaghetti meatballs – a bowl of pasta and vegetables can get boring so these are great to jazz it up to make a tasty accompaniment to salad. Definitely one to impress your friends – this dish is perfect for a dinner party and goes really well with a glass of red wine (or two).

MEATBALLS WITH *Tomato & Basil Sauce*

SERVES 4–6

3 tbsp olive oil

1 large onion, finely chopped

100g mushrooms, finely chopped

2 garlic cloves, finely chopped

200g smoked tofu, finely diced

1 large carrot, grated

8 sage leaves, finely chopped

1 small handful of flat-leaf
   parsley leaves, roughly chopped,
   plus extra chopped parsley to
   garnish

100g mixed nuts, such as hazelnuts, pecan nuts and walnuts

400g can brown lentils, drained
   and rinsed

400g can green lentils, drained
   and rinsed

100g plain flour, for dusting

3–4 tbsp olive oil, for shallow frying

Sea salt and freshly ground
   black pepper

Grated vegan Parmesan cheese
   and finely chopped flat-leaf
   parsley, to serve

For the easy tomato sauce:

680g passata

400g can chopped tomatoes

2 tbsp extra virgin olive oil

1 tsp dried oregano

1 small handful of basil leaves,
   roughly chopped

Heat the oil in a large non-stick saucepan over a medium heat, add the onion and cook for 5 minutes or until softened and translucent. Add the mushrooms, garlic and tofu, and cook for 5–6 minutes. Add the carrot and sage, and cook for 3 minutes. Remove from the heat and stir in the parsley. Leave to cool for a few minutes.

Meanwhile, put the nuts in a small pan and toast them over a medium-high heat for 1–2 minutes or until evenly toasted, shaking the pan frequently. Tip onto a plate and leave to cool. Transfer to a food processor and whizz until finely chopped. Tip the nuts into a large mixing bowl, then add half the green and brown lentils.

Put the mushroom mixture into the food processor with the remaining lentils. Pulse the mixture until it comes together – you want it to blend together but still retain some texture. Add this to the mixing bowl. Season with salt and pepper, and mix well with your hands.

Roll golf-ball sized pieces of the mixture and put onto a baking tray. Put them in the fridge for 1 hour to set.

Meanwhile, put all the tomato sauce ingredients in a saucepan with 100ml water over a medium-high heat. Bring to the boil, then reduce the heat and gently simmer for 15 minutes. Season the sauce with salt and pepper.

Dust the meatballs lightly with flour, shaking off any excess. Heat the oil in a large non-stick frying pan and cook the meatballs on all sides until well browned. Pour most of the tomato sauce into bowls, add the meatballs and spoon a little more sauce over the top. Sprinkle with Parmesan and parsley, then serve.

When you think shepherd's pie, you think warm and comforting. It's the ultimate in winter fare and the kind of thing you can easily freeze and warm up throughout a week – if you can hold back enough to have leftovers! I've replaced the mince with lentils and lots of veggies. The herbs really make it, and the topping is deliciously creamy. The nutritional yeast is what gives the topping an extra nutty taste – along with your favourite vegan cheese sprinkled on top so it can go nice and crispy in the oven. Guilt-free all the way through, which makes tucking in that little bit more satisfying.

Shepherd's PIE

SERVES 6–8

2 tbsp olive oil

1 onion, finely chopped

2 carrots, finely chopped

3 celery sticks, finely chopped

2 garlic cloves

1 tbsp thyme leaves

1 tbsp ground cumin

1 tbsp tomato purée

400g can chopped tomatoes

1 tbsp vegan Worcestershire
   sauce

250ml vegetable stock

3 × 400g cans lentils,
   drained and rinsed

½ tbsp dried mixed herbs

Sea salt and freshly ground
   black pepper

1 tbsp finely chopped flat-leaf
   parsley leaves, to garnish

For the potato and swede mash:

700g potatoes, cut into chunks

500g swede, cut into chunks

75g vegan butter, plus
   2 tbsp extra

75ml soya milk

3 tbsp nutritional yeast

150g vegan cheese, grated

Preheat the oven to 220°C (200°C fan, gas 7). Heat the oil in a large non-stick saucepan, add the onion and cook for 5 minutes, or until softened and translucent. Put in the carrots, celery, garlic and thyme, and cook for 5 minutes. Add the cumin, stir and cook for 1 minute, then add the tomato purée. Stir and cook for 1 minute.

Add the tomatoes, Worcestershire sauce, stock, lentils and mixed herbs, then stir well. Season with salt and pepper, then bring the mixture to the boil. Reduce the heat and simmer for 15 minutes.

Meanwhile, to make the topping, put the potatoes and swede in a large saucepan. Cover with cold water and add 1 tsp salt. Bring to the boil, then reduce the heat and simmer for 15–20 minutes or until soft. Drain in a colander. Return to the pan and mash with a potato masher until smooth.

Stir in the 75g butter until melted. Return the pan to a gentle heat and stir in the milk, nutritional yeast and cheese. Season and stir well until the cheese begins to melt, then remove from the heat.

Pour the lentils into a deep 25 × 30cm baking dish. Top with spoonfuls of the swede mash. Spread out the mash evenly over the lentils. Finish by dotting the mash with the 2 tbsp butter.

Cook on the top shelf of the oven for 20 minutes or until the mash is crispy and golden brown. Serve garnished with parsley.

You no longer have to feel left out at Sunday roast! Why should you have to miss out? You shouldn't! There have been so many occasions in restaurants where people have just served me a plate of veggies, but Sunday is one of those days when you want to eat to your heart's content. However, after trying this recipe you may not want to reserve it just for Sundays . . . The nuts and mushrooms have a meaty texture to them and the filling is packed with flavour. I would serve this with roasted veg and your favourite sauces.

Butternut Squash & Sage NUT ROAST

SERVES 4–6

800g butternut squash,
    cut into 2.5cm chunks
2 tbsp olive oil
250g mixed nuts – I use
    pecans, blanched almonds
    and walnuts
300g chestnut mushrooms,
    halved
1 onion, finely chopped
2 garlic cloves, finely chopped
1 handful of sage leaves,
    finely chopped
180g cooked chestnuts,
    roughly chopped
50g natural dried
    breadcrumbs
Sea salt and freshly ground
    black pepper

For the topping:
1 tbsp olive oil
A handful of sage leaves
30g dried cranberries
40g cooked chestnuts, halved

Preheat the oven to 180°C (160°C fan, gas 4) and grease a 900g non-stick loaf tin. Put the butternut squash onto a baking tray and add 1 tbsp of the oil, then season with salt and pepper. Mix well, then cook in the oven for 30 minutes. Meanwhile, put the nuts in a small pan and toast them over a medium-high heat for 1–2 minutes or until evenly toasted, shaking the pan frequently. Tip out of the pan onto a plate and leave to one side.

Meanwhile, put the mushrooms in a food processor and pulse until they are finely chopped.

Heat the remaining oil in a large saucepan, add the onion and cook for 5 minutes, or until softened and translucent. Add the garlic and cook for 2 minutes, then add the mushrooms. Cook until all the liquid has evaporated. Add the sage and chestnuts, stir well and cook for 2 minutes, then remove from the heat.

Put the nuts in the food processor and pulse until finely chopped. Add these to the mushroom mixture. Remove the butternut squash from the oven and mash roughly with a fork. Add this to the mushroom mixture followed by the breadcrumbs. Combine well, season to taste and spoon into the prepared loaf tin. Cook in the oven for 30 minutes. Remove from oven and leave to cool in the tin for 5 minutes.

Meanwhile, to make the topping, heat the oil in a frying pan over a medium-high heat and fry the sage leaves for 2–3 seconds until crisp. Remove from the pan. Mix together the topping ingredients in a bowl. Turn the roast out of the loaf tin onto a serving dish and sprinkle the topping over the roast. Cut into thick slices to serve.

One that anyone who loves mild curries will enjoy. The coconut milk and cream replace double cream and are much better for you. Plus, I think the sweet edge makes this curry taste even better. You could have it with rice, on its own or with some delicious naan bread. I like to scoop the curry on the naan bread and enjoy it that way.

Sweet Potato & Kale CURRY

SERVES 4

2 tbsp vegetable oil

1 onion, finely diced

2.5cm piece of fresh root
   ginger, peeled and grated

2 garlic cloves, finely chopped

4 cardamom pods

1 tsp ground turmeric

1 tsp sea salt

750g sweet potatoes,
   cut into 2.5cm chunks

400ml vegetable stock

400ml coconut milk

80g red lentils

150ml coconut cream

3 large handfuls of kale,
   cut into bite-sized pieces

100g roasted unsalted
   cashew nuts

Basmati rice, to serve

For the curry powder:

1 tsp black mustard seeds

1 tsp fenugreek seeds

1 tsp cumin seeds

1 tsp fennel seeds

1 tbsp coriander seeds

1 small handful of dried
   curry leaves

To make the curry powder, measure out a scant level teaspoon or tablespoon of each spice. Put all the ingredients for the curry powder into a small frying pan over a low heat. Toast the spices gently for 5 minutes or until they become fragrant. Don't over-toast them or let them brown too much or the curry powder will be overly strong and bitter.

Remove from heat and leave to cool. Grind in a coffee grinder or pestle and mortar until fine. Leave to one side.

Heat the oil in a large saucepan over a medium heat and cook the onion for 8 minutes or until softened and beginning to brown. Next, put in the ginger and garlic, and cook for 2 minutes. Add the cardamom pods, turmeric, curry powder and salt. Stir for 30 seconds, then add the sweet potatoes, stock, coconut milk and lentils. Stir well, then cover and bring to the boil. Reduce the heat and simmer for 15 minutes.

Stir the curry well and add the coconut cream and kale. Cook for 5 minutes, then stir in half the cashew nuts. Serve the curry, sprinkled with the remaining nuts, with basmati rice.

I'm a sucker for Indian food (especially on a Sunday night) but struggle to find takeaways that can do a curry without cream, which can be frustrating. So I've got into making them at home instead, and it's really straightforward! It turns out that the coconut cream tastes SO much nicer and it's better for you. This mild and creamy curry won't disappoint.

Chickpea & Butternut Squash CURRY

SERVES 2

2 tbsp vegetable oil

6 cardamom pods, split

8 curry leaves

1 tsp black mustard seeds

1 large onion, finely chopped

2 garlic cloves, finely chopped

2.5cm piece of fresh root
ginger, peeled and grated

1 tsp ground turmeric

1 tsp ground cumin

1 tsp ground coriander

½ tsp sea salt

500ml vegetable stock

400g butternut squash,
cut into 2.5cm chunks

250ml coconut cream

400g can chickpeas, drained
and rinsed

2 handfuls of baby spinach

Brown rice and poppadoms,
to serve

Heat the oil in a saucepan over a high heat. Add the cardamom, curry leaves and mustard seeds, then stir and cook for 30 seconds. Reduce the heat to medium. Add the onion and cook for 8 minutes until softened and beginning to brown.

Put in the garlic and ginger, and cook for 2 minutes. Add the turmeric, cumin, coriander and salt, then cook for 1 minute. Pour in the vegetable stock and bring to the boil. Add the butternut squash, return to the boil, then reduce the heat and simmer for 10 minutes.

Add the coconut cream and chickpeas, then cook for 10 minutes or until the curry thickens slightly. Remove from the heat and stir in the spinach. Spoon the curry into bowls and serve with steaming-hot brown rice and poppadoms.

Kormas are my all-time favourite curry! I used to get them every Sunday, along with pilau rice and poppadum with mango chutney. When I went vegan I realised I couldn't get veg kormas (or pilau rice!) any more as they pretty much all use cream. This one is soooo easy to make, you may get addicted. The cashews blend with this so well and give it that extra crunch, as everything else is relatively soft. I hope you love it as much as I do – curry Sundays are back!

Vegetable KORMA

SERVES 2

2 tbsp oil
½ large onion, finely chopped
2 garlic cloves, finely grated
2.5cm piece of fresh root
   ginger, peeled and
   finely grated
1 tsp medium curry powder
1 tsp garam masala
1 tsp ground turmeric
1 tsp sea salt
100g tomatoes, finely chopped
400ml can coconut milk
2 tbsp desiccated coconut
100g carrot, diced
100g mixed broccoli and
   cauliflower, cut into
   small florets
100g courgette, cut into
   small chunks
100g green beans, trimmed
   and cut into 2.5cm pieces
60g roasted and salted
   cashew nuts
2 tbsp vegan yogurt
Chopped coriander leaves,
   to garnish

Heat the oil in a large non-stick saucepan over a high heat. Add the onion and cook for 5-7 minutes or until softened and beginning to brown. Reduce the heat to medium. Add the garlic and ginger, and cook for 2 minutes. Put in the curry powder, garam masala, turmeric and salt, and cook for 1 minute. Add the tomatoes and cook for 1-2 minutes or until the mixture forms a paste.

Add the coconut milk, 150ml water, the desiccated coconut and carrot. Bring to the boil, then reduce the heat and simmer for 5 minutes. Add the remaining vegetables and cook for a further 10 minutes. Remove from the heat.

Chop half the cashew nuts and add to the pan followed by the yogurt. Stir well and serve in bowls. Top with the remaining cashew nuts and the coriander.

I love using chickpeas as an alternative to meat as they are substantial and high in protein. The curry will help fill in the void of your usual tikka masala, and you could also add chicken replacements such as vegan Quorn. This is such a satisfying meal and quick to whip up at home.

CHICKPEA *Tikka Masala*

SERVES 4

1 tbsp light olive oil

1 large red onion, cut into
   large dice

1 red pepper, deseeded and
   cut into large dice

1 green pepper, deseeded
   and cut into large dice

150g cauliflower, cut into
   small florets

4 tbsp tikka masala
   spice paste

2 400g cans chickpeas,
   drained and rinsed

400g can chopped tomatoes

400ml can coconut milk

Sea salt and freshly ground
   black pepper

Coriander leaves, to garnish

Chapattis or pilau rice,
   to serve

Heat the oil in a large saucepan over a medium-high heat. Add the onion and a pinch of salt, and cook for 3–4 minutes, or until softened and translucent, stirring occasionally. Tip in the peppers and cook for 1 minute.

Add the cauliflower and tikka masala paste, and cook for 1 minute or until fragrant. Next, put in the chickpeas, tomatoes, 100ml water and half the can of coconut milk. Bring to the boil, then reduce the heat, season to taste and simmer for 15 minutes.

Pour in the remaining coconut milk and cook for a further 5 minutes. Serve sprinkled with coriander and with chapattis or pilau rice alongside.

Another Asian dish that is a particular favourite of mine. However, I discovered only recently that a lot of places make pad thai with a fish sauce, so even vegetable pad thai could be off the menu! The good news is that fish sauce is actually quite easy to recreate by infusing the tamarind paste and soy sauce. I've added in lots of different veggies so this dish with all its colours and textures looks incredible – and tastes even better!

Pad THAI

SERVES 1

100g dried flat rice noodles
1 tbsp soy sauce
1 tbsp tamarind paste
1 tbsp light muscovado sugar
1 tbsp vegetable oil
1 garlic clove, finely chopped
2.5cm piece of fresh root
    ginger, peeled and cut
    into thin strips
½ red onion, thinly sliced
¼ tsp ground turmeric
100g firm tofu, crumbled
120g prepared stir-fry
    vegetable mix (such as
    carrots, beansprouts,
    Asian greens, etc.)
1 tbsp chopped peanuts and
    chopped coriander leaves,
    to garnish
2 lime wedges, to serve

Soak the noodles in cold water for 10 minutes or until soft. Put the soy sauce, tamarind and sugar in a bowl and mix together, then leave to one side.

Put a non-stick wok over a high heat. When hot, add the oil, garlic and ginger, and cook for 30 seconds. Add the onion, turmeric and tofu, and stir-fry for 4–5 minutes or until the tofu becomes crispy.

Add the vegetable mix and stir-fry for 2 minutes. Lift the noodles out of the water and put directly into the wok. Stir-fry for 2 minutes, then add the tamarind sauce mix and 2 tbsp water. Stir-fry for another 2–3 minutes or until the noodles are soft and coated in the thickened liquid, then garnish with peanuts and coriander. Serve with lime wedges.

Feed Me
SWEET
TREATS

*R*eally simple to make and the ideal substitute for your favourite chocolate bar. These are much healthier and gluten free, which makes them taste even sweeter.

Chocolate & Coconut BARS

MAKES 15

250g desiccated coconut
250ml coconut cream
3–4 tbsp agave syrup
1 tsp vanilla paste
250g vegan chocolate,
    chopped
2 tbsp coconut oil

For the decoration:
Nibbed pistachio nuts
Dried rose petals
Toasted coconut flakes

Line a baking tray with greaseproof paper. Put the desiccated coconut into a food processor and pulse 2 or 3 times. Add the coconut cream, agave and vanilla paste. Pulse again until well combined.

Take heaped tablespoonfuls of the mixture and form them into 2.5cm × 7.5cm long bars. Put them onto the prepared tray. Put into the freezer for 30 minutes to set.

Melt the chocolate and coconut oil in a heatproof bowl over a pan of gently simmering water, making sure the base of the bowl doesn't touch the water. Stir occasionally. Remove from the heat and leave to cool for 5 minutes.

Take a coconut bar and dip it quickly into the chocolate. Using two forks, lift it out of the chocolate and let the extra chocolate drip away. Put the bar back onto the lined tray and sprinkle with some of the pistachio nuts, rose petals or coconut flakes. Repeat with the remaining bars and put in the fridge to set for 30 minutes.

*Q*uick and easy, and one of my healthier sweet bites, these are the ideal snack. I like to have them post-gym or if I want a sweet something after a meal. Try them out with your friends – they'll love them too.

BAD-ASS *Bliss Balls*

MAKES 30

150g vegan gingernut biscuits
150g plain Hobnob biscuits
100g pitted dried dates,
  finely chopped
75g desiccated coconut
50g cocoa powder
150g crunchy peanut butter
100ml coconut oil, melted

For the coatings:
50g cocoa
50g desiccated coconut
20g freeze-dried raspberries,
  lightly crushed

Line a baking tray with greaseproof paper. Crush the biscuits by putting them in a plastic bag and bashing them with a rolling pin until they turn into crumbs. (Alternatively, you can put them into a food processor and pulse to turn them into crumbs.) Put the crumbs in a bowl.

Pulse the dates in a food processor until they are finely chopped, or chop them finely using a sharp knife. Add them to the bowl with the desiccated coconut, then add the cocoa, peanut butter and coconut oil. Using both your hands, mix all the ingredients together – don't be tempted to do this with a spoon, you really must use your hands!

Once everything is mixed well, add 3 tbsp water and mix again until the mixture is wet and sticky. Put the ingredients for the coatings into three shallow bowls. Roll the mixture into small golf-ball sized balls. As you roll them, drop them into one of the bowls of toppings. Once you have 4 balls in the bowl, shake the bowl around until all the balls are coated.

Put them onto the prepared baking tray and transfer to the fridge for 30 minutes or until set.

Chocolate & Pecan COOKIES

MAKES 24

50g pecan nuts
2 tbsp ground flaxseed
110g coconut oil
2 tsp vanilla extract
110g light muscovado sugar
50g icing sugar
½ tsp bicarbonate of soda
1 tsp baking powder
120g vegan chocolate chips
200g plain flour

Preheat the oven to 200°C (180°C fan, gas 6) and line two baking trays with greaseproof paper. Put the pecan nuts in a small pan and toast them over a medium-high heat for 1–2 minutes or until evenly toasted, shaking the pan frequently. Tip out of the pan onto a plate. Leave to cool and chop finely. Leave to one side.

Put the flaxseed in a small bowl and mix with 5 tbsp water. Stir well and leave for 5 minutes to soak.

Put the coconut oil into a mixing bowl and add the vanilla extract, sugar, icing sugar and soaked flaxseed. Using an electric whisk, whisk for 2 minutes or until creamy.

Fold in the bicarbonate of soda, baking powder, pecan nuts, chocolate chips and flour. Mix until just combined.

Put heaped tablespoonfuls of the cookie dough onto the prepared baking trays. Bake for 10–12 minutes or until lightly golden. Cool on wire racks – they are also delicious served warm!

If you feel like treating a loved one with something to satisfy a sugar craving then these are really cute! It was really disappointing when shop-bought dodgers turned from being vegan-friendly to not . . . So this recipe allows you to keep them in your life! You can use your favourite jams, and have some fun experimenting with different shapes!

Jam BISCUITS

MAKES 16

150g vegan butter

100g light soft brown sugar

3 tbsp golden syrup

½ tbsp vanilla paste

360g plain flour, plus extra
  for dusting

1 tsp bicarbonate of soda

½ tsp fine sea salt

1 tbsp soya milk, if needed

Assorted jams, such as
  raspberry, blackcurrant,
  apricot and strawberry

Icing sugar, for dusting

Line two baking trays with greaseproof paper. Put the butter in a large mixing bowl and add the sugar, golden syrup and vanilla paste. Whisk together until soft and creamy. Add the flour, bicarbonate of soda and salt, then stir well until the mixture comes together. It's easier to use your hands at this point. If it's a little dry, add a dash of milk.

Once the dough has come together, flatten it a little and wrap it in clingfilm, then transfer it to the fridge for 1-2 hours until very firm.

Remove from the fridge. Take a large piece of greaseproof paper and dust it lightly with flour. Put the dough on top and roll it out to about 3mm thickness. Using a 6cm round fluted cookie cutter, cut out 32 rounds and put them onto the prepared baking trays. Using mini cookie cutters, cut shapes from the middle of 16 of the cookies. (Alternatively, cut out shapes using a small, sharp knife.) Put in the fridge for 15 minutes. Preheat the oven to 200°C (180°C fan, gas 6).

Put both trays in the oven for 6-8 minutes or until the biscuits turn a light golden brown. Remove from the oven and allow them to cool on the trays. Take the biscuits and flip them all over. Add a heaped teaspoon of your favourite jam onto each biscuit without the hole. Top with a biscuit with a hole and press down gently. Dust with icing sugar to finish.

I never used to be a fan of cheesecake pre-veganism, but since making the change I was intrigued to see what dairy-free cheesecake would taste like. I was pleasantly surprised; it's creamy and tasty but not too rich. I found some bases really dry and I didn't enjoy the texture, but this particular base is a little bit chewy and crunchy at the same time – much more enjoyable. Although indulgent, this cheesecake is healthier than the usual, while still managing to fulfil that sweet craving.

MINI *Blueberry Cheesecakes*

MAKES 12

300g cashew nuts
125g walnuts
250g pitted dried dates,
    roughly chopped
Sunflower oil spray
Zest and juice of 1 lemon
1 tbsp vanilla extract
125ml maple syrup
125ml coconut milk
3 tbsp coconut oil
300g blueberries
2 tbsp maple syrup

Put the cashew nuts in a bowl and cover with boiling water. Leave to soak for 1 hour. Put the walnuts and dates into a food processor and blend until the mixture comes together and everything is finely chopped. Grease each cup of a deep 12-cup muffin tray with the sunflower oil spray. Divide the walnut mixture among the 12 cups and press down firmly. Put into the freezer for 10 minutes to firm up quickly.

Drain the cashew nuts and put them into the cleaned food processor with the lemon zest and juice, the vanilla, maple syrup, coconut milk and coconut oil. Blend until completely smooth. Divide the filling among the muffin cups and put them in the freezer for 20–30 minutes until hard.

Blend 225g of the blueberries and the maple syrup together until completely smooth. Spoon a little over each cheesecake and spread it out so that it's even. Return to the freezer for 30 minutes. Cover with clingfilm and freeze for 3 hours.

When the cheesecakes are completely frozen, remove the tray from the freezer and, using a palette knife, lift them out of the muffin tray. Put them on a serving plate and leave them to soften for about 20 minutes. Sprinkle a few of the remaining blueberries on top of each one to decorate, and serve.

These are ridiculously easy to make: simply mix all the ingredients together and pop them in the fridge! Rocky road is hugely popular and I totally get why – it has so many different types of crunchiness and sweetness in a bar. Vegan marshmallows are easy to find these days and are delicious. Just try and get any friends to tell the difference.

Rocky ROAD

MAKES ABOUT 14

300g vegan chocolate

2 tbsp coconut oil

200g vegan mini
marshmallows

75g salted peanuts

75g dried sour cherries

10g salted popcorn

100g vegan digestive biscuits,
broken into small pieces

1 tbsp dried rose petals

Line the base of a 20cm square tin with two layers of clingfilm. Melt the chocolate and coconut oil in a heatproof bowl over a pan of gently simmering water, making sure the base of the bowl doesn't touch the water. Stir occasionally. Remove from the heat and leave to cool for 5 minutes.

Put the marshmallows, peanuts, cherries, popcorn and biscuits in a large mixing bowl. Pour in the chocolate and mix well until everything is coated. Tip into the prepared tin and press down well with the back of a spoon. Sprinkle with dried rose petals. Put into the freezer for 2 hours to set, then remove and cut into large squares to serve.

I used to love going camping with my dad and sister, and there's nothing better than hot marshmallows on the fire, or delicious s'mores! However, most marshmallows contain gelatine, so it's lucky that the vegan alternatives taste so good! These are really quick and easy to make and you don't have to miss out on sweet treats while camping.

S'mores

MAKES 4

8 vegan chocolate
   digestive biscuits
120g vegan mini
   marshmallows

Preheat the oven to 220°C (200°C fan, gas 7) and line a baking tray with greaseproof paper. Put 4 digestive biscuits on the prepared baking tray, chocolate-side up. Put a cookie cutter the same size as your digestive on top of the biscuit. Fill with marshmallows and top with another digestive, chocolate side down. Carefully lift the cookie cutter off and repeat with the remaining biscuits.

Bake on the top shelf of the oven for 2–3 minutes or until the marshmallows puff up and brown well. (Alternatively, use a blowtorch and run it over the marshmallows until they are well browned.) Wait for about 20 seconds so that you don't burn your mouth – and then tuck in!

Sweet and tangy and surprisingly soft – a pudding for all those citrus lovers out there. The main substance of the slice contains superfoods such as coconut and almonds, which are particularly good for your skin and hair.

Lemon & Coconut SLICES ————————

MAKES 12

150g blanched almonds
250g pitted dried dates,
   halved
1 tsp vanilla paste
Zest and juice of 2 lemons
220g desiccated coconut
½ tsp sea salt

For the topping:
100g vegan butter
200g icing sugar
1 tsp lemon extract
Zest of 1 lemon

Line the base of a 900g loaf tin with two layers of clingfilm. Put the almonds in a food processor and whizz until they resemble fine crumbs. Add the dates and blend again until the dates are finely chopped.

Add the vanilla paste, lemon zest and juice, coconut and salt, then pulse until the mixture comes together.

Tip the mixture into the tin and press down and flatten with a spoon. Cover with clingfilm and put in the fridge for 2 hours.

Meanwhile, make the buttercream for the topping. Put the butter in a bowl and beat it with a wooden spoon until soft. Add the icing sugar and the lemon extract and beat again. Spoon into a piping bag.

Remove the loaf tin from the fridge. Lift the cake out of the tin and remove the clingfilm. Cut the cake into 12 even slices. Pipe a little buttercream onto each slice and sprinkle with lemon zest.

Flapjacks are one of those sweet treats that are ideal on the go. I love making a batch and then snacking on them throughout the week, or giving some to friends and family and basking in their praise. Since becoming vegan I struggle to find flapjacks when I'm out and about because they all use butter. One of those situations where you look at the ingredients, just in case, only to be disappointed time and time again. So the best solution – make your own! You can leave these plain if you like, but the coconut and apricot add an extra bit of sweetness.

Coconut & Apricot FLAPJACKS

MAKES 12–14

200g vegan butter
200ml golden syrup
150g soft light brown sugar
250g rolled oats
75g desiccated coconut
100g pumpkin seeds or
    mixed seeds
200g dried apricots,
    finely chopped

Preheat the oven to 200°C (180°C fan, gas 6) and line a 20 × 25cm baking tin with greaseproof paper.

Put the butter in a small saucepan and add the golden syrup and sugar. Put the pan over a medium heat and stir until the butter has melted and the sugar has dissolved. Remove from the heat.

Put the rolled oats in a large bowl and add the coconut, pumpkin seeds and apricots. Stir well, add the butter mixture and stir again until everything is coated. Spoon the mixture into the lined baking tin. Press the mixture down evenly with the back of a spoon.

Bake on the bottom shelf for 25–30 minutes or until golden brown. Leave to cool in the tin for 15 minutes before cutting into bars.

I used to order milkshakes pretty much everywhere I went, even getting them delivered to my house. (Seriously, if you don't believe me just scroll through my Instagram page – the evidence is all there.) Luckily, milkshakes can still be enjoyed on a vegan diet and, once again, you won't even notice the difference. I made this one with protein powder, which means it's perfect for pre- or post-gym, or even if you just want a boost.

Chocolate & Banana MILKSHAKE

SERVES 1

1 banana, cut into chunks
    and frozen
2 tbsp Hershey's chocolate
    syrup
1 tbsp vegan chocolate
    protein powder
160ml almond milk
1 scoop vegan chocolate
    ice cream
A small handful of ice cubes
Cocoa, for dusting

Put the frozen banana into a blender or food processor and add 1 tbsp of the syrup, the protein powder, almond milk and chocolate ice cream. Blend until smooth.

Pour the remaining syrup around the inside of a serving glass. Add the ice cubes to the glass and pour the milkshake into the glass. Dust with a little cocoa and serve.

Sundae? Surely not? Funnily enough, ice cream is something you really don't have to sacrifice when going vegan. There are SO many amazing vegan ice cream brands out there and I would go as far as saying they are actually better than dairy ice cream. Mostly made with banana or coconut, they are creamy and delicious, so ice cream is still on the menu!

BANANA BERRY *Nice Cream Sundae*

SERVES 1

1 banana, cut into chunks
    and frozen
70g frozen mixed berries
1 tbsp maple syrup
1–2 tbsp coconut milk
2 scoops of vegan vanilla
    ice cream
80g fresh mixed berries, such
    as strawberries, raspberries
    and blueberries
Vegan squirty cream
Vegan ice cream wafer

Put the banana into a blender or food processor and add the frozen berries, maple syrup and coconut milk. Blend until smooth. You might need to scrape down the sides with a rubber spatula and blend twice to make sure it's blended properly.

Put one-third of the fresh berries in a sundae glass. Top with half the berry mixture. Add a scoop of vanilla ice cream, more berry mixture, fresh berries and another scoop of vanilla ice cream.

Top with a good amount of squirty cream and decorate with the remaining berries. Serve with a wafer.

*O*reo milkshakes were always my absolute
favourite and the very best news is that Oreos
are actually VEGAN. I was so pleased when I realised
that I wouldn't have to give them up – there are a few
snack foods you might be surprised to find are vegan,
so keep an eye out. This is sooooo easy to make, so if
you're in the mood for a lazy pudding vibe then get the
Oreos at the ready!

Oreo THICKSHAKE

SERVES 1

5 Oreo cookies
3 scoops of vegan vanilla
    ice cream
120ml almond milk
2 tbsp Hershey's chocolate
    syrup
Vegan squirty cream

Put 3 of the Oreos into a blender or food processor
with the ice cream, half the syrup and almond milk.
Blend until smooth. Drizzle the remaining chocolate
syrup into the serving glass, then pour the shake in and
top with a good amount of squirty cream. Cut 1 Oreo in
half and crush one half over the cream. Use the other
$1^1/_2$ Oreos as a decoration.

A recipe that any new vegans or curious vegan wannabes out there may think is off the menu forever. Veganism is all about sacrifice, right? Wrong. This book is really about showing you how much you can still indulge yourself while following a vegan lifestyle. Vegan chocolate is, to me, more delicious than dairy chocolate. For a recipe like this soya milk is my favourite – I find it is most similar to cows' milk. Who doesn't want a tasty hot chocolate on a cold winter's night or even just for a pick-me-up?

HOT *Chocolate*

SERVES 1

250ml soya milk
1 tbsp good-quality cocoa
¼ tsp ground cinnamon
50g vegan chocolate, grated,
   plus extra for decoration
1 tbsp golden caster sugar
1 tbsp amaretto
2 tbsp vegan Baileys
   Irish Cream
Vegan squirty cream
Biscuits, to serve

Put the soya milk into a small non-stick saucepan over a medium heat and bring to a gentle simmer. Add the cocoa, cinnamon, grated chocolate and sugar, and stir well until the sugar has dissolved.

Stir in the amaretto and Baileys, and pour into a mug. Top with lashings of squirty cream and grated chocolate. Enjoy with your favourite biscuits.

Feed Me
CAKE

This cake is so incredible that I really can't tell if it's vegan or not. It tastes exactly the same as a non-vegan one! Having experimented with vegan baking, and knowing how cruel the farming industries can be, I now don't understand why people bother using eggs in recipes at all. They are completely unnecessary. If you love chocolate cake as much as I do (i.e. a lot) then this recipe will not disappoint.

TWO-LAYER
Chocolate Fudge Cake

SERVES 12–16

Sunflower oil spray,
    for greasing
250g self-raising flour
1 tsp baking powder
½ tsp sea salt
200g demerara sugar
120g light muscovado sugar
120g good-quality cocoa
    powder
550ml soya milk
1 tbsp vanilla extract
2 tsp apple cider vinegar
90ml vegetable oil
Fresh strawberries and extra
    melted vegan chocolate,
    to decorate

For the chocolate fudge icing:
300g good-quality vegan
    dark chocolate, chopped
225g vegan butter
300g icing sugar
A large pinch of fine sea salt

Preheat the oven to 200°C (180°C fan, gas 6), and grease and line two 20cm round loose-based cake tins with greaseproof paper. Sift the flour, baking powder and salt into a large mixing bowl. Stir in both the sugars and the cocoa. Heat the milk in a small saucepan over a medium heat until it just comes to a simmer. Remove from the heat and stir in the vanilla, vinegar and oil. Mix well.

Make a well in the dry ingredients and gradually whisk in the milk. Whisk until the mixture is smooth and lump-free. Divide the cake batter between the prepared tins.

Put the tins on a baking sheet and bake in the centre of the oven for 25 minutes or until a skewer inserted into the centre comes out clean. If there is cake mix on the skewer, return the cakes to the oven for 5 minutes more.

Allow to cool in the tins for 5 minutes, then remove from the tins and put on a wire rack to cool completely.

To make the fudge icing, melt the chocolate in a heatproof bowl over a pan of gently simmering water, making sure the base of the bowl doesn't touch the water. Stir occasionally. Remove from the heat.

Put the butter in a bowl and add the icing sugar and salt. Cream them together using an electric whisk. Pour in the chocolate while it is still warm so that it combines well into the icing.

Flip one cake over onto a serving plate so that you have a flat surface. Working quickly, spread one-third of the icing onto the cake. Top with the second cake and cover the top and sides with the remaining icing. If you leave it too long the chocolate will set and it will be harder for you to spread the icing. Decorate with some fresh strawberries and a drizzling of melted vegan chocolate. This cake is lovely and moist, so it will last for four or five days in the fridge.

T his is the kind of cake I would want at my wedding one day. Light, fluffy, creamy and truly irresistible. It's not the kind of recipe anyone would ever associate with a vegan diet but once you've tried it you'll realise anything is possible in vegan cooking.

Victoria Sponge CAKE

SERVES 12

250g vegan butter
250g golden caster sugar
1 tbsp vanilla extract
Zest of 1 lemon
300g vegan yogurt
275ml soya milk
6 tsp baking powder
400g plain flour

For the filling:
200g vegan butter
350g icing sugar, plus extra
    for dusting
5 tbsp raspberry jam
250g fresh raspberries

Preheat the oven to 200°C (180°C fan, gas 6) and line two 20cm round loose-based sponge tins with greaseproof paper. Put the butter in a bowl and add the sugar and vanilla. Cream together using an electric whisk for 2 minutes or until soft and creamy. Fold in the lemon zest.

Whisk the yogurt and milk together in a separate jug, then leave to one side. Sift the baking powder and flour into the bowl and slowly stir in the yogurt mixture. Once everything has been incorporated give it a quick whisk to ensure the cake batter is smooth.

Divide the mixture between the prepared tins. Bake in the centre of the oven for 25–30 minutes until cooked through and a skewer inserted into the centre comes out clean. If there is cake mix on the skewer, return the sponges to the oven for 5 minutes more. Leave to cool in the tins for 10 minutes, then invert the sponges onto wire racks to cool completely.

To make the buttercream for the filling, put the butter in a bowl and add the icing sugar. Using an electric whisk, whisk together until soft and creamy. Put the buttercream into a piping bag with a medium round nozzle. Put one cake on a serving plate and spoon the raspberry jam on top. Spread it evenly to the edges using a palette knife. Pipe large dots of buttercream in an even layer on top of the jam.

Pop the other cake on top and put the raspberries in the middle of the top cake. Sprinkle with icing sugar and serve.

These brownies are to die for. This is a seriously dangerous recipe because once they're ready to eat, it's hard to stop. It's also impressive to make for friends when you want to be able to say '. . . and they're vegan!', and of course are essential if you have a sweet tooth. They take no time at all and look so pretty, so make sure you have your phone ready to show off #whatveganseat.

Chocolate & Raspberry BROWNIES

MAKES 16

200g vegan chocolate,
    chopped into small chunks
170g golden caster sugar
80g vegan butter
190g self-raising flour
3 tbsp cocoa powder
240ml soya milk
A pinch of sea salt
1 tsp vanilla extract
150g raspberries
20g nibbed pistachio nuts

Preheat the oven to 200°C (180°C fan, gas 6) and line a 20cm square baking tin with greaseproof paper. Melt 150g of the chocolate with the sugar and butter in a heatproof bowl over a pan of gently simmering water, making sure the base of the bowl doesn't touch the water. Gently stir while the mixture begins to melt and the sugar dissolves – this should take about 5 minutes. Remove the bowl from the heat.

Sift the flour and cocoa into a large mixing bowl. Add the milk, salt, vanilla and the chocolate mixture. Stir well until completely combined. Add half the raspberries and the remaining chocolate chunks to the bowl and stir gently.

Pour the mixture into the prepared baking tin. Sprinkle with the remaining raspberries and the pistachio nuts. Bake in the centre of the oven for 20–25 minutes until set but still soft. The brownies will continue to cook in the tin once you remove them from the oven, so be careful not to overcook them. You still want them to be a bit gooey in the middle. Remove from oven and cool in the tin for 15 minutes. Cut into squares and serve.

Not everyone out there loves chocolate cake so this is a perfect alternative, and a bit of a lighter option. The tang of the lemon alongside the crunch of the pistachios is a great combination. It's nearly impossible to taste the difference when using soya yogurt. You don't need eggs to make a cake as is proven by this recipe – the fluffiness is all there.

Lemon & Yogurt LOAF CAKE

SERVES 10

Sunflower oil spray,
   for greasing
300g plain flour
1 tsp baking powder
1 tsp bicarbonate of soda
½ tsp salt
140g golden caster sugar
Zest and juice of 2 lemons
130ml light olive oil
280ml vanilla soya yogurt
1 tbsp vanilla extract
50g vegan butter, melted
Zest of 1 lemon, for decoration
25g pistachio nuts,
   roughly chopped

For the yogurt icing:
250g icing sugar
3 tbsp vanilla soya yogurt

Preheat the oven to 180°C (160°C fan, gas 4) and grease a non-stick loaf tin with oil spray. Sift the flour, baking powder, bicarbonate of soda and salt into a large mixing bowl. Add the sugar and lemon zest, and mix well.

Put the olive oil in a bowl and add the yogurt, vanilla and melted butter. Whisk until smooth. Stir into the dry ingredients until well combined, then whisk in the lemon juice.

Pour the cake batter into the prepared tin and bake on the lower shelf of the oven for 35–40 minutes until cooked through and a skewer inserted into the centre comes out clean. If there is cake mix on the skewer, return the loaf to the oven for 5–10 minutes more.

Leave to cool in the tin for 10 minutes. Remove the cake from the tin and leave on a wire rack to cool completely.

To make the icing, sift the icing sugar into a bowl, then whisk in the yogurt. Spread the cake with the icing. Sprinkle with lemon zest and pistachio nuts. Slice and serve.

I'm obsessed with cupcakes – they're one of those things that are really fun to make if you're in the baking mood! The icing for these is next level. You can get really creative if you want to, the options are endless. Apple cider vinegar also has many proven health benefits. The most common way of getting more of it in your diet is diluting a tablespoon of the vinegar with a large glass of water so once you've added this to your pantry you could even experiment with adding it to your everyday routine.

Vanilla & Passion Fruit CUPCAKES

MAKES 12

250ml soya milk
1 tsp apple cider vinegar
140g vegan butter
220g golden caster sugar
1 tbsp vanilla paste
2 tsp baking powder
½ tsp fine sea salt
250g plain flour

For the passion fruit buttercream:
150g vegan butter
300g icing sugar
1 tsp vanilla extract
2 passion fruits, halved

Preheat the oven to 200°C (180°C fan, gas 6) and line a deep 12-cup muffin tin with paper muffin cases. Pour the milk and cider vinegar into a small bowl. Stir well and leave for 2 minutes to curdle slightly.

Put the butter, sugar and vanilla paste in a large mixing bowl. Using an electric whisk, whisk for 2 minutes or until creamy.

Add the baking powder and salt to the bowl. Add half the milk mixture and sift in half the flour, then mix well with a wooden spoon. Add the remaining milk mixture and flour, and mix again.

Divide the mixture among the muffin cases. Bake for 20 minutes, then leave on a wire rack to cool completely.

To make the buttercream, put the butter, icing sugar and vanilla extract in a bowl and whisk until smooth and creamy. Spoon out the pulp from each passion fruit, then add the pulp to the icing and mix well. (If you'd rather have a coloured buttercream icing, omit the passion fruit and mix with a little of your favourite food colouring paste instead.)

Put a little of the buttercream on the top of each cupcake, then swirl the top with the back of a spoon.

If you feel in the mood to impress people with a showstopper of a pudding then this is the one to go for. Coconut cream means it is (technically) healthier which makes it soooo much easier to serve yourself a slightly larger slice. I have to say I prefer this recipe to the original – it tastes lighter but is still so scrumptious. Though it's difficult to be patient, make sure you give the base time to set: you don't want it crumbling as you slice, however keen you are to get stuck in . . .

Banoffee PIE

SERVES 10–12

400ml can coconut milk
1 tsp vanilla extract
100g soft dark brown sugar
A large pinch of salt
150g plain Hobnob biscuits
150g vegan digestive biscuits
100g vegan butter, melted

For the filling:
3 × 250ml packs of coconut
    cream
40g vegan dark chocolate,
    grated
2–3 ripe bananas, as needed,
    thickly sliced

Pour the coconut milk into a small saucepan over a medium heat and add the vanilla extract, sugar and salt, then bring the mixture up to the boil and reduce the heat to simmer gently for 20–25 minutes until reduced and syrupy, stirring occasionally. Leave this caramel mixture to cool, then put it in the fridge for 1–2 hours to firm up.

Crush both types of biscuits by putting them in a plastic bag and bashing them with a rolling pin until they turn into crumbs. (Alternatively, you can put them into a food processor and pulse to turn them into crumbs.) Tip into a bowl and pour the melted butter over the top. Mix well and then tip the mixture into a 23cm loose-based tart tin. Using your fingers, push the biscuits right up the edges of the tin. Use the bottom of a glass to press the mixture evenly down over the base. Put in the fridge for 1 hour to set.

To make the filling, open each pack of coconut cream and drain out the watery liquid. Put in a bowl and stir together.

Sprinkle half the dark chocolate over the biscuit base to cover. Pour over the caramel mixture and spread to the edges evenly. Next, lay the banana slices on top in a single layer. Top with spoonfuls of the coconut cream and make a few swirls using a spoon. Sprinkle over the remaining chocolate. Leave the pie in the fridge until you are ready to serve.

A traditional comforting dish, perfect for those evenings when you just need some pie. The pastry is straightforward to make, but if you want an even easier version, you can cheat and use Jus-Rol shortcrust pastry – it's vegan friendly!

Apple PIE

SERVES 10–12

200g vegan butter, plus extra
    for greasing
475g plain flour
200g icing sugar
8 Granny Smith apples
Juice of 1 lemon
150g golden caster sugar,
    plus 2 tbsp extra
100g sultanas
½ tsp ground mixed spice
½ tsp ground cinnamon
4 tbsp vegan butter
2 tbsp soya milk

Preheat the oven to 220°C (200°C fan, gas 7) and grease a deep 23cm pie dish with vegan butter.

Sift the flour and icing sugar into a large mixing bowl. Add the butter and rub it into the flour using your fingertips until it resembles coarse breadcrumbs – work quickly so that it doesn't get too greasy. Add 1–2 tbsp cold water, as needed, to the bowl and bring the mixture together to form a dough. Wrap in clingfilm and chill in the fridge for 20 minutes.

Meanwhile, peel and core the apples. Cut into 1cm-thick wedges and put into a large bowl. Squeeze over the lemon juice and mix well. Add the 150g sugar, the sultanas, mixed spice and cinnamon, then combine well.

Melt the butter in a large saucepan over a medium heat, add the apple mixture and cook for 10 minutes or until the apples have softened but still retain their shape. Pour the mixture onto a tray and leave it to cool completely.

Cut one-third of the dough and leave it to one side. Roll out the larger piece between two pieces of greaseproof paper into a 30cm round. Gently lift off the top piece of greaseproof paper and invert the dough into the pie dish. Take off the second piece of paper. If there any cracks in the dough, just patch them up with any offcuts of pastry. Put this in the fridge to keep cool.

Roll out the other piece of dough into a 26cm round in the same way. Take the pie dish out of the fridge, and fill it with the cooled apple filling. Put the pastry circle on top and trim the edges.

Cut some decorative leaves from the offcuts of pastry, if you like. Brush the top with milk, and lay the leaves decoratively over the top of the pie, then brush them with milk as well. Sprinkle with the 2 tbsp sugar and bake on the lower shelf of the oven for 30–40 minutes until golden and crispy. Remove from oven and leave it to cool for 10 minutes before serving.

Who doesn't love an apple crumble? For me it's a classic pudding and was one of the first recipes I remember making with my mother. We'd use the apples from the trees in our garden and forage for blackberries, or substitute rhubarb if they weren't in season. It was so simple to make this recipe vegan-friendly and it tastes the same as the original! Great for using up old apples and for dinner with friends – serve with some vegan custard or ice cream!

Apple & Blackberry CRUMBLE

SERVES 4–6

750g Bramley apples
500g Granny Smith apples
Juice of 2 lemons
300g blackberries
100g demerara sugar
1 tsp ground mixed spice
100g vegan butter, melted
Vegan ice cream, to serve

For the crumble topping:
250g plain flour
180g vegan butter cut into
   1cm cubes
60g Demerara sugar
125g rolled oats

Preheat the oven to 200°C (180°C fan, gas 6). Prepare the apples by peeling them and removing the cores. Cut them into 2.5cm chunks and put them into a large mixing bowl. Pour the lemon juice over them and mix well to coat.

Add the blackberries, sugar, mixed spice and melted butter to the bowl. Mix well and transfer to a non-stick 25 × 30cm baking dish.

To make the topping, sift the flour into a bowl and add the butter. Rub the mixture together using your fingertips until it resembles coarse crumbs. Stir in the sugar and rolled oats. Mix well, then sprinkle the crumble topping over the apple mixture. Bake for 30 minutes or until the topping turns golden brown and the apples are cooked. Remove from the oven and leave to cool slightly before serving with lots of vanilla ice cream.

One of my favourite sweet treats pre-veganism, I would happily order a box of 12 Krispy Kremes on a casual weekday and nail them with a friend or my sister. Giving them up was obviously massively beneficial to my health, not to mention my waistline! However, doughnuts are one of those things that it seems slightly unreasonable to never ever eat again. A face full of sugar and a mouth full of jam – who doesn't want that?! With this recipe, you can have both, along with a clean conscience to help you sleep at night. This recipe takes time and maybe a tad more effort than some of the others, but trust me it's 100 per cent worth it!

Hot Cinnamon
JAM DOUGHNUTS

MAKES 15–18

7g sachet dried yeast

1 tbsp golden caster sugar, plus 60g

40g vegan butter, melted

1 tsp vanilla extract

400g plain flour, plus extra for dusting

½ tsp baking powder

½ tsp ground cinnamon

Light olive oil, for greasing and shallow frying

180g raspberry jam

For the cinnamon dusting:

200g golden caster sugar

1 heaped tsp ground cinnamon

Line a baking tray with greaseproof paper. Put 240ml warm water in a small bowl and add the yeast and the 1 tbsp sugar. Stir to mix, then leave for 5–10 minutes to activate and become frothy.

Put the butter in a small bowl and add the vanilla. Stir well to combine. Sift the flour, baking powder and cinnamon into a large mixing bowl and stir in the 60g sugar. Make a well in the centre. Pour in the yeast mixture and the butter mixture, and stir well until the mixture comes together to form a dough.

Remove from the bowl and knead the dough on a lightly floured work surface for 3–4 minutes until smooth. Clean out the bowl and lightly grease it with a little olive oil. Put the dough back in the bowl and cover with clingfilm. Put the bowl in a warm place for 1 hour or until the dough doubles in size.

Roll out the dough on a lightly floured work surface until 2.5cm thick. Using a 5cm plain round cookie cutter, cut out rounds and put them onto the prepared tray. Leave for 15 minutes to rise.

To make the cinnamon dusting, put the sugar in a mixing bowl and add the cinnamon. Mix well.

Heat oil to a depth of 5–7.5cm in a large saucepan or deep-fat fryer to 170°C (test by frying a small cube of bread; it should brown in about 60 seconds). Lower the dough circles 5 or 6 at a time (depending on the size of your saucepan) carefully into the oil and cook for 2–3 minutes on each side. They will puff up and turn golden brown. Remove from the oil and drain on kitchen paper, then put them into the cinnamon dusting and coat well all over.

Put some jam into a piping bag. Poke a hole into each doughnut using a skewer or chopstick, then pipe a little jam into each doughnut. Serve while still hot.

The only response I've had when I've made these is 'wow'. Everyone I know who has ever tried them is obsessed. You really can have them at any time of the day and they are so fluffy and doughy, they pretty much melt in your mouth.

Cinnamon BUNS

MAKES 16

250g strong white bread flour,
    plus extra for dusting
250g plain flour
1 tbsp caster sugar
1 tsp salt
7g sachet fast-action dried
    yeast
150ml soya milk,
    at room temperature
1 tsp egg replacer
50g vegan butter, softened,
    plus extra for greasing

For the filling:
100g vegan butter
80g light brown muscovado
    sugar
25g flour
2 tbsp ground cinnamon

For the cinnamon icing:
100g icing sugar
¼ tsp ground cinnamon

Put the flours in a large mixing bowl and add the sugar, salt and yeast. Stir well. Add 120ml water, at room temperature, and the milk. Mix the egg replacer with 2 tbsp water (or follow the pack instructions to make 1 egg), and mix this into the bowl. Stir well with a wooden spoon. Squeeze the softened butter in with your hands until it's all incorporated.

Knead the dough for 5–10 minutes or until smooth and elastic – it will be a bit sticky, but don't add any flour as yet. All the butter will incorporate into the dough as you knead it. Put into a greased bowl, cover with clingfilm and put in a warm place for 1 hour or until doubled in size.

In the meantime make the filling by mixing all the ingredients together in a bowl. Preheat the oven to 220°C (200°C fan, gas 7) and grease a 24 × 34cm baking tray.

Dust the work surface with flour and tip the dough out onto the flour. Roll the dough into a 40 × 50cm rectangle and spread the filling evenly over the dough. Roll up the dough tightly from the closest long end to you, and roll until you have a long cylinder. Trim off the end part and then slice the dough into 16 even pieces.

Lay the dough pieces on the prepared baking tray and leave to rest for 20–30 minutes until they have risen slightly. Bake on the top shelf of the oven for 15–20 minutes until golden.

Meanwhile, to make the icing, put the icing sugar and cinnamon in a bowl and stir in enough water to give the mixture the consistency of golden syrup. Remove the buns from the oven and leave to cool for 5 minutes. Remove from the tin and put on a wire rack to cool completely. Drizzle with the icing and leave to set.

Feed Me

SNACKS
& SIDES

Hearty and filling – these nachos are comfort food at its very best! Adding the vegan mince turns them into a dish that you'll really want to get stuck into – great if you want a big sharing dish for a group of friends, or if you're having a movie night. Make sure you refer to my chilli con queso recipe (page 155) for this one – it's perfect for getting messy and dipping into!

Nachos

SERVES 2 AS A MAIN OR 4 AS A SNACK

2 tbsp light olive oil
1 small onion, chopped
2 garlic cloves, finely chopped
1 tsp ground cumin
1 tsp paprika
½ tsp dried oregano
1 tsp sea salt
500g frozen vegan mince
400g can chopped tomatoes
400g can red kidney beans,
    drained and rinsed

To serve:
250g tortilla chips
200ml chilli con queso
    (see page 155)
1 tomato, diced
3 spring onions, sliced
Coriander leaves,
    roughly chopped

Preheat the oven to 200°C (180°C fan, gas 6). Heat the oil in a saucepan over a medium-high heat. Add the onion and cook for 5-7 minutes or until softened and beginning to brown. Add the garlic and cook for 1 minute, stirring frequently. Sprinkle in the cumin, paprika, oregano and salt, and stir well.

Add the vegan mince, chopped tomatoes and kidney beans with 250ml water. Bring the mixture to the boil, then reduce the heat and simmer gently for 10 minutes.

Meanwhile, warm the tortilla chips in the oven for 3-4 minutes until toasted and golden. Heat up the chilli con queso in a small saucepan, and add a little boiling water if the mixture is too thick.

Put the tortilla chips on a serving dish. Spoon the chilli con queso over the tortilla chips. Spoon over the mince and sprinkle with tomato, spring onions and coriander. Serve immediately.

*A*nother delightful discovery was that puff pastry is vegan (refer to the Store Cupboard for more info)! So it's very easy to make vegan pasties and tarts, and they taste pretty much identical to any non-vegan favourites. This galette is great for a lunch with some salad, or if you're having an outdoor picnic or BBQ it is perfect to add to the spread. I for one am always last minute with everything so if you are in a rush or feeling a bit lazy I'd recommend this . . .

Griddled Courgette GALETTE

SERVES 6

500g block Jus-Rol puff pastry

500g courgettes, thickly sliced
    on the diagonal

3 tbsp extra virgin olive oil,
    plus extra to drizzle

100g vegan cream cheese

30g sun-dried tomato paste

1 tbsp soya milk

70g sun-blush tomatoes,
    roughly chopped

Sea salt and freshly ground
    black pepper

2 tbsp dill leaves, to garnish

Preheat the oven to 220°C (200°C fan, gas 7) and line a baking sheet with greaseproof paper. Roll the pastry out to 20 × 30cm. Trim the edges so that it's a neat rectangle. Using a sharp knife, score an inner rectangle 2cm in from the edge. Prick the inside of the rectangle all over with a fork, then put the pastry onto the prepared baking sheet and put it in the fridge. Leave it there while you prepare the topping.

Put the courgette slices in a large bowl. Add the oil and season with salt and pepper, then mix well. Heat a large griddle pan over a high heat and, when hot, carefully add some of the courgette slices in a single layer. Cook for 1–2 minutes on each side until lightly charred. Remove the courgettes from the pan and put onto a plate. Repeat with the remaining courgette slices.

Mix the cream cheese and tomato paste together into a bowl. Season the mixture with salt and pepper.

Take the pastry from the fridge and spread the cream cheese mixture evenly over the inside rectangle. Lay the courgettes over and season with a little salt. Brush the edges of the pastry with the milk.

Bake on the centre shelf of the oven for 10 minutes. Then sprinkle with the chopped sun-blush tomatoes and return to the oven for a further 15 minutes.

Remove from the oven and drizzle with extra virgin olive oil. Sprinkle with fresh dill and serve.

When ordering rice dishes from takeaways you'll be surprised by how many aren't vegan friendly. Like pilau rice for instance, or egg fried rice. Rice options are surprisingly limited unless you go for plain old boiled rice, which can get a bit boring. Sometimes it's nice to spice your rice up a bit and this goes with so many savoury options. I like to have it with vegan Quorn chicken and soy sauce if I'm looking for a quick supper.

Fried RICE

SERVES 4

70g uncooked, or 250g
   cooked and cooled,
   jasmine rice
1½ tbsp vegetable oil
1½ tbsp sesame oil
2 garlic cloves, finely chopped
2 spring onions, finely sliced
1 small courgette,
   finely chopped
100g broccoli, finely sliced
1 handful of kale,
   finely chopped
50g frozen peas
2 tbsp soy sauce
3 tbsp nutritional yeast
A pinch of ground
   white pepper
Roughly chopped coriander
   leaves and toasted sesame
   seeds, to garnish

It is very important to prepare your rice properly. Put it in a large bowl and cover generously with cold water, then use your hand to swish the rice around to release the starch. Drain in a strainer and repeat twice more. Pour boiling water into a large saucepan and return to the boil over a high heat. Add the rice, stir once, then reduce the heat to low and simmer, partially covered, for 10–15 minutes until cooked. Drain in a strainer and rinse with cold water. Drain again, then transfer to a tray, spread it out and leave it to cool, then put it into the fridge to cool completely. Once that's done, you can start cooking!

Put a wok over a very high heat. When it is very hot, add the oils, garlic and spring onions. Stir-fry for 1 minute then add the courgette and broccoli. Cook for 1 minute more.

Add the kale and peas, and stir-fry for 1 minute, then add the rice. Stir well and cook for 3–4 minutes until heated through. Add the soy sauce and 1 tbsp water, the nutritional yeast and pepper. Stir-fry for another 2–3 minutes. Serve in bowls garnished with coriander and sesame seeds.

*P*lant-based junk food at its best, with no compensating on flavour! Corn chips are one of my favourite savoury treats and this dip is the perfect sidekick for them. It's totally moreish and you won't be able to stop digging in. You will need to have a blender at the ready, though that's something you won't regret buying as it comes in useful for so many recipes!

CHILLI *Con Queso*

MAKES ABOUT 500ML

5 tbsp light olive oil
½ large onion, thinly sliced
2 garlic cloves, thinly sliced
1 green jalapeño chilli,
   deseeded and sliced
½ tsp garlic salt
½ tsp ground turmeric
1 tsp paprika
120g potatoes, very
   thinly sliced
140g roasted cashew nuts
150ml soya milk
2 tbsp nutritional yeast
1 tsp sea salt

Heat the oil in a saucepan over a medium heat. Add the onion, garlic and chilli, and cook for 8 minutes or until softened and just beginning to brown, stirring frequently.

Put in the garlic salt, turmeric and paprika, and cook for 30 seconds or until fragrant. Add the potatoes, cashew nuts, 150ml water and the milk, and bring to the boil. Reduce the heat and simmer for 10–15 minutes until the potatoes are completely tender.

Remove from heat and stir in the nutritional yeast and salt. Transfer the mixture to a powerful blender and add 2–4 tbsp boiling water, as needed, to loosen the mixture. Blend on high speed for 1–2 minutes or until completely smooth. If the mixture is too thick, add more boiling water. If the mixture isn't completely smooth, pass it through a sieve for a better consistency. Warm through before serving.

You can use this as a dip for corn chips or as a base 'cheese' sauce for nachos (see page 150).

One of the simpler recipes, but as it's a favourite I wanted to include it. I wanted this book to not only introduce you to some amazing recipes, but also be a place to turn to when you're stuck for quick recipe inspiration, a feeling that I'm sure many of you are familiar with. Avocado and cheese toasties were a favourite of mine before I gave up cheese and thought I had lost them forever, until I discovered Violife! It's my favourite type of vegan cheese for toasties – it melts really well and is great with avo. If you haven't tried it already you have to give it a go! Ideal for lunch or breakfast if you're in a rush, or if you're just feeling a bit lazy.

AVOCADO *Grilled Cheese Toastie* ———

SERVES 1

2 thick slices sourdough
  bread, toasted
1 tbsp vegan butter
1 tsp white miso paste
2 slices Violife vegan
  Cheddar cheese
½ ripe avocado, pitted
1 handful of alfalfa sprouts
Sea salt and freshly ground
  black pepper

Preheat the oven to 180°C (160°C fan, gas 4) with grill element on. If you are using a separate grill, preheat it to medium.

Spread each piece of warm toast with butter. Spread one slice with miso paste and put one slice of cheese on each slice of toast. Put the toast onto a baking tray. Grill for 2–3 minutes until the cheese has melted.

Scoop the flesh from the avocado using a tablespoon and slice it thickly. Lay the avocado on one slice of toast and top with alfalfa. Season the other slice with salt and pepper and put on the top. Press down and serve.

I really wanted to find a vegan alternative to creamed kale as when I see it on menus I get jealous. This version is exactly what you would hope for! Kale doesn't always need to be boring, and this is an ideal side for pretty much anything.

Creamed KALE

SERVES 2

2 tbsp vegan butter

2 garlic cloves, finely chopped

A pinch of chilli flakes,
    plus extra to garnish

140g kale, cut into bite-sized
    pieces

150ml single soya cream

2 tbsp nutritional yeast

A pinch of grated nutmeg

Sea salt and freshly ground
    black pepper

Melt the vegan butter in a non-stick saucepan over a medium heat. Add the garlic and chilli flakes, and cook for 1 minute.

Add the kale to the pan with 3 tbsp water and cook for 2 minutes, stirring frequently. Add the cream, nutritional yeast, nutmeg, and salt and pepper. Stir well and cook for 3–4 minutes or until the kale has softened and the cream has thickened. Serve sprinkled with chilli flakes.

One of the prettiest recipes, these are really very healthy and perfect for snacking on. The peanut dip is everything, it completes the dish. Quick and easy to make, ideal for a bite in the day or as a starter to impress your friends – there are so many reasons why these should become a favourite recipe! You can include pretty much whatever veggies you choose, but the smoked tofu is particularly great for adding flavour.

Rainbow Rice Paper Rolls
WITH PEANUT DIP

MAKES 8

8 Vietnamese rice papers
1 long red chilli, thinly sliced
　　on the diagonal
8 mint leaves
1 small carrot, cut into
　　thin strips
150g cucumber, cut into
　　thin strips
150g red cabbage,
　　thinly shredded
½ red pepper, deseeded
　　and cut into thin strips
½ yellow pepper, deseeded
　　and cut into thin strips
200g smoked tofu, cut into
　　thin strips
1 handful of coriander leaves
40g salted roasted peanuts

For the peanut dip:
2 tsp sesame oil
2 tbsp crunchy peanut butter
1 tbsp tahini
1 tbsp soy sauce
2 tbsp water
2 tbsp coconut milk
1 tsp palm sugar

To make the peanut dip, put all the ingredients in a small saucepan over a low heat and stir until the sauce has warmed through and has come together. Leave to one side.

Wet each round of rice paper under cold water until it has begun to soften. Lay flat on the work surface. Put 2 slices of chilli in the middle of the rice paper and top with a mint leaf. Divide the remaining ingredients into eight portions and put one portion of each into the centre of the rice paper. Fold the 2 edges inwards over the filling and then roll the rest up tightly to make one neat roll. Repeat with the remaining 7 rice papers.

Spoon the peanut dip into a serving bowl and serve alongside the rice paper rolls for dipping.

Sometimes it really is the simple things in life that make us happy and this Mexican side can do just that. It is ideal for a BBQ – try it alongside one of my vegan burgers and you'll realise you're not missing out on anything.

MEXICAN CORN *with Chipotle Crema*

MAKES 4

4 corn cobs
30g vegan Parmesan cheese,
    finely grated
1 tbsp coriander leaves,
    roughly chopped
Smoked paprika, to sprinkle
4 lime wedges, to serve

For the chipotle crema:
120g silken tofu
1 small garlic clove, crushed
1 tsp apple cider vinegar
Mustard
60ml soya milk
100ml light olive oil
100ml extra virgin olive oil
2 tbsp chipotle chillies
    in adobo
Sea salt and freshly ground
    black pepper

Put the corn cobs in a large saucepan, cover with water and sprinkle with salt. Bring to the boil over a high heat, then reduce to a simmer. Cook for 25–30 minutes or until tender. Drain.

Meanwhile, to make the chipotle crema, put the tofu, garlic, vinegar, mustard and milk into a blender or food processor. Whizz until smooth. Put both the oils in a jug. Turn the blender back on and slowly pour the oil into the blender while the machine is still running.

Transfer the crema to a bowl and stir in the chipotle, then season with salt and pepper.

Spread the chipotle crema all over each corn cob. Sprinkle with Parmesan, coriander and smoked paprika and serve with lime wedges.

If you don't like mushrooms, then, let's be honest, this one isn't for you! But if like me you're a fan then these are an impressive starter or side dish and go with pretty much anything. The vegan cream cheese is really similar to the dairy version – Sheese does a really nice one.

Stuffed MUSHROOMS

SERVES 2

6 large mushrooms,
    stalks removed
80g vegan garlic and herb
    soft cheese
3 tbsp plain flour, plus 80g
4–5 tbsp soya milk
150g dried breadcrumbs
Light olive oil, for shallow
    frying
Sea salt and freshly ground
    black pepper
1 handful of rocket leaves,
    dressed in a little lemon
    juice and olive oil, to serve

For the sauce:
2 tbsp olive oil
100g mushrooms,
    thickly sliced
100g fresh tomatoes,
    finely chopped
1 tsp tomato purée
6 basil leaves, finely chopped
3 tbsp soya cream

Preheat the oven to 200°C (180°C fan, gas 6). Fill the mushrooms with the soft cheese. In a bowl, make a batter by whisking together the 3 tbsp flour with the milk – you want a smooth, slightly thick batter.

Put the 80g flour in a shallow bowl and the breadcrumbs in another bowl. Dip a mushroom in the flour, making sure it's well coated, and dust off any excess. Using a fork, dip it into the batter, then lift it out and drop it into the breadcrumbs. Coat the mushroom well with the breadcrumbs – it's very important not to leave any holes, or the cheese will escape during cooking.

To make the sauce, heat the oil in a small frying pan, add the mushrooms and cook for 5 minutes or until they begin to brown. Add the tomatoes, tomato purée and 4 tbsp water. Season with salt and pepper and simmer gently for 3–4 minutes until the sauce has thickened. Put the sauce into a small food processor with the basil leaves and blend until smooth. Return to the frying pan and add the soya cream. Stir well and keep the sauce warm.

Heat enough oil for shallow frying the mushrooms in a frying pan to 170°C (test by frying a small cube of bread; it should brown in about 60 seconds). Put the mushrooms into the oil and cook for 2–3 minutes on each side until golden. Remove and drain the mushrooms on kitchen paper. Transfer them to a baking tray, filling-side up, and cook in the oven for 5 minutes.

Pour the sauce into the middle of each plate. Top each plate with 3 mushrooms and serve with a few dressed rocket leaves.

These gyozas are surprisingly meaty for a vegan dish! The sweet and salty flavours of Asian cuisine can still be enjoyed while following a vegan diet, which is great for variation. These would be a perfect side dish, or served as a starter. Why not team them with something like the Fried Rice (see page 154)?

Miso Aubergine & Mushroom
GYOZAS

MAKES 14

½ × quantity Miso-Glazed
   Aubergine (page 39)
2 tbsp vegetable oil
100g chestnut mushrooms,
   finely diced
1 large garlic clove, crushed
1 tbsp soy sauce
2 spring onions, finely sliced
A pinch of white pepper
14 gyoza skins
Finely sliced green part of a
   spring onion, and toasted
   sesame seeds, to garnish

For the dipping sauce:
1½ tbsp black rice vinegar
1 tbsp soy sauce
½ tsp sesame oil

Line a baking tray with greaseproof paper. Scrape the flesh from the aubergine then dice it finely. Put it into a bowl.

Heat 1 tbsp of the oil in a frying pan. Add the mushrooms and cook for 3–4 minutes until browned. Add the garlic and cook for 1 minute, then add the soy sauce and cook until the liquid has evaporated.

Remove the pan from the heat and stir in the spring onions and white pepper. Add this mushroom mixture to the bowl with the aubergine and stir well. Leave to cool.

Put a teaspoon of the aubergine mixture into the centre of each gyoza skin. Wet your finger and wet half the edge of the gyoza skin, then bring the 2 sides together and pinch and fold the skin from one end to the other. Press down firmly so that it's well sealed, as you don't want the filling to come out during cooking. Put onto the prepared baking tray as you go.

To make the dipping sauce, mix all the ingredients together in a serving dish.

Heat the remaining oil in a large, lidded, non-stick frying pan over a medium heat. When the oil is hot, add the gyozas flat-side down and cook for 2–3 minutes until the flat side is a deep golden brown and crispy. Add 80ml water, then cover and cook for 2–3 minutes until the gyoza skin has steam-cooked. Remove the lid and let the remaining water evaporate. Cook for 2 minutes or until the flat sides of the gyozas are crispy again.

Garnish with a sprinkling of spring onion and sesame seeds, and serve with the dipping sauce.

These have so much flavour and the cool avocado cream complements them deliciously. I like to whip up a batch in the evening if I'm watching TV or to pass round as a starter at a dinner party. The chilli gives them a good kick!

Corn & Green Chilli POPPERS

MAKES 10–12

1 tsp egg replacer
320g canned sweetcorn,
   drained
¼ tsp paprika
1 tsp baking powder
3 tbsp cornflour
40g plain flour
1 green jalapeño chilli,
   with seeds, finely diced
1 spring onion, finely diced
1 tbsp finely chopped
   coriander leaves
Light olive oil, for deep-frying
Sea salt and freshly ground
   black pepper

For the avocado cream:
1 ripe avocado, halved
   and pitted
Juice of ½ lime
2 tbsp vegan mayonnaise
1 tbsp finely chopped
   coriander leaves

Put the egg replacer in a small bowl and mix with 2 tbsp water. Put 250g of the corn in a blender or food processor and add the egg replacer liquid, the paprika and baking powder. Whizz until smooth. Stir in the cornflour, plain flour, chilli, spring onion, coriander and remaining corn. Season with salt and pepper and stir well. Leave it to stand for 10 minutes.

To make the avocado cream, scoop the flesh from the avocado into a bowl using a tablespoon. Add the lime juice and mash together with a fork until completely smooth. Add the mayonnaise and a pinch of salt and pepper. Mix again and leave to one side.

Heat 5cm oil in a saucepan to 170˚C (test by frying a small cube of bread; it should brown in 60 seconds).

Drop tablespoonfuls of the corn mixture into the oil, making sure not to overcrowd the pan. Cook for 2 minutes on one side or until golden brown, then flip them over and cook for another 2 minutes on the other side. Remove them from the oil and drain on kitchen paper, then sprinkle them with a little salt. Repeat with the remaining mixture. Serve the poppers hot with the avocado cream for dipping.

The perfect snack for when you're watching a movie at home or you've decided to have a BBQ. The seasoning is everything with this recipe and you'll be surprised by how 'meaty' the cauliflower is!

Cauliflower WINGS

SERVES 2

1 cauliflower, broken into
   small florets
4 tbsp maple syrup
3 tbsp soy sauce
2 tbsp mirin
4 tbsp nutritional yeast
½ tsp onion powder
½ tsp garlic powder
¼ tsp cayenne pepper

To serve:
1 tbsp toasted sesame seeds
2 spring onions, green part
   only, thinly sliced on
   the diagonal
Hot sauce (optional)

Preheat the oven to 200°C (180°C fan, gas 6) and line a baking tray with greaseproof paper. Put the cauliflower in a mixing bowl. Add the maple syrup, soy sauce, mirin, nutritional yeast, onion powder, garlic powder and cayenne pepper. Mix well and leave to marinate for 20 minutes.

Remove the cauliflower from the marinade and put it onto the prepared baking tray. Reserve the marinade. Cook the cauliflower on the top shelf of the oven for 20 minutes.

Meanwhile, pour the marinade into a small saucepan and cook over a medium heat to reduce it by half or until syrupy to make a glaze. Remove the cauliflower from the oven and baste it with the glaze, then return it to the oven for 5 minutes. Remove from the oven and put it on a plate. Sprinkle with sesame seeds and spring onions and serve with a little hot sauce, if you like it spicy.

The ultimate in homemade junk food! Sometimes people associate tofu with being tasteless but in this recipe it replaces the chicken so well! The seasoning here is the key to making tofu great. Or greater.

TOFU *Popcorn Chicken*

SERVES 2

200g firm tofu
140g chickpea (gram) flour
4 tbsp nutritional yeast
1 tsp Cajun seasoning
1 tbsp finely chopped flat-leaf
   parsley leaves
Light olive oil, for deep-frying
Sea salt and freshly ground
   black pepper
Hot sauce and celery sticks,
   to serve

For the ranch dressing:
4 tbsp vegan mayonnaise
½ tsp Dijon mustard
¼ tsp dried dill
A pinch of dried thyme
A pinch of onion powder
A squeeze of lemon juice
2 tsp soya milk

Dry the tofu well with kitchen paper, then break it into bite-sized pieces and dry them again. Leave to one side.

Put the chickpea flour in a mixing bowl and add the nutritional yeast, Cajun seasoning and parsley. Season with salt and pepper. Whisk in 150ml water until the batter is smooth.

Make the ranch dressing by mixing together all the ingredients in a small serving bowl, then leave to one side.

Heat the oil to a depth of 5cm in a non-stick saucepan or deep-fat fryer to 180°C (test by frying a small cube of bread; it should brown in 60 seconds). Add the tofu to the batter and coat each piece well using two forks, then drop them into the oil carefully and cook for 4–5 minutes or until the batter is golden and crispy. Do this in two batches so that you don't overcrowd the pan. Remove from the oil and drain on kitchen paper. Sprinkle with a little salt. Repeat with the remaining tofu.

Serve with the ranch dressing and the hot sauce in another bowl for dipping, with some crispy celery sticks alongside.

The crispy outer texture mixed with the gooey centre makes these a total delight. They're a great alternative to processed snacks.

Courgette CHIPS

SERVES 2

Light olive oil, for deep-frying

128g pack tempura batter mix

¼ tsp smoked paprika,
   plus extra to sprinkle

1 tsp garlic salt

1 tbsp finely chopped flat-leaf
   parsley leaves

Zest of 1 lemon, plus extra
   to sprinkle

180ml ice-cold sparkling water

2 courgettes, thickly sliced
   on the diagonal

30g vegan Greek-style cheese,
   crumbled

Sea salt and freshly ground
   black pepper

Heat the oil to a depth of 5cm in a non-stick saucepan or deep-fat fryer to 180˚C (test by frying a small cube of bread; it should brown in 60 seconds). Put the tempura mix in a bowl and add the smoked paprika, garlic salt, parsley, lemon zest, and salt and pepper.

Whisk in the sparkling water, until just combined – don't over-mix! Add the courgette slices to the bowl and coat each one well, then drop them carefully into the oil using two forks. Do this in two batches so that you don't overcrowd the pan. Cook for 2–3 minutes until golden on one side and then flip them over to cook the other side. Remove them from the pan and drain on kitchen paper. Sprinkle with a little sea salt and repeat with the remaining courgette slices.

Put the courgette chips onto a serving plate and sprinkle with the Greek-style cheese. Add a pinch of smoked paprika and lemon zest, and devour these crispy morsels while they are hot!

Perfect for jazzing up a boring dish or using as a sandwich filler with some veggies. Or if you simply want a more exciting dip than hummus!

Romesco SAUCE

SERVES 4

3 large red peppers
2 large ripe tomatoes
40g blanched almonds,
   toasted
1 tbsp light olive oil
40g stale bread, torn into
   bite-sized pieces
2 garlic cloves, sliced
½ tsp smoked paprika,
   plus extra to sprinkle
1 tbsp sherry vinegar
100ml extra virgin olive oil
Sea salt and freshly ground
   black pepper

Preheat the oven to 240°C (220°C fan, gas 9). Put the peppers and tomatoes on a baking tray. Cook on the top shelf of the oven for 12 minutes. The skin should have slightly charred and blistered. Remove from the oven and tip into a bowl. Cover with clingfilm and leave to cool.

Meanwhile, put the almonds in a small pan and toast them over a medium-high heat for 1–2 minutes or until evenly toasted, shaking the pan frequently. Tip out of the pan onto a plate and leave to one side.

Remove the clingfilm from the bowl and carefully peel the skin off each pepper, then remove the seeds. Put the flesh into a blender or food processor. Remove the skin from the tomatoes and add them to the blender.

Heat the light oil in a small frying pan, add the bread, and toast for 2 minutes or until the bread is beginning to turn golden brown. Add the garlic, cook for 30 seconds and then remove the pan from the heat. Tip the bread into the food processor followed by the paprika, almonds, vinegar and extra virgin olive oil. Add a good pinch of salt and some pepper. Blend until smooth. Serve in a bowl, sprinkled with a little smoked paprika. Good served with barbecued or roasted Mediterranean vegetables.

Really simple to make, it tastes EXACTLY the same as the original and is a favourite for dipping with bread or French fries.

Roasted Garlic AIOLI

MAKES 350ML

4 large garlic cloves, unpeeled
1 tsp olive oil
120g silken tofu
1 heaped tsp Dijon mustard
2 tsp apple cider vinegar
60ml soya milk
100ml light olive oil
100ml extra virgin olive oil
Sea salt and freshly ground
    black pepper

Preheat the oven to 180°C (160°C fan, gas 4). Pour the 1 tsp of olive oil over the garlic cloves, then wrap them in foil and cook in the oven for 15 minutes. The skin should be browned and the garlic flesh nice and soft. Leave to cool.

Remove the garlic skins and put the roasted flesh into a small food processor. Add the tofu, mustard, vinegar and milk. Add a good pinch of salt and pepper.

Turn the food processor on and slowly pour in the oils until the mixture emulsifies. If it begins to get too thick, loosen it with a little warm water. Spoon into a jar and keep it in the fridge until needed. It will keep for 2–3 days.

Mushroom is one of those 'meatier' vegetables and mixed with the right flavours makes a delicious pâté. Pâté is not something I'd ever really eaten, until I came across this mushroom version. I am a big bread lover so it's perfect for a bit of a carb fix! This takes just 10 minutes to make – though you will need your trusty food processor. Great served as a starter with bread or as a light snack with some seeded crackers.

Mushroom PÂTÉ

SERVES 4

3 tbsp vegan butter
1 small onion, finely chopped
2 garlic cloves, sliced
400g chestnut mushrooms,
    quartered
180g cooked chestnuts
1 tsp thyme leaves
40ml Pedro Ximenez
2 tbsp soy sauce
2 tbsp porcini mushroom paste
1 tbsp red wine vinegar
2 tbsp flat-leaf parsley leaves
4 thyme sprigs and about
    100g vegan butter, melted
    (optional)
Sea salt and freshly ground
    black pepper
Sourdough toast, to serve

Heat the butter in a large saucepan over a high heat. Add the onion and the garlic, and cook for 3–4 minutes or until the onion is softened and translucent.

Add the mushrooms, chestnuts and thyme leaves, and cook for 6–8 minutes until the mushrooms have browned well. Season with salt and pepper.

Pour in the Pedro Ximenez and stir well until the liquid has completely evaporated. Then add the soy sauce and porcini paste. Stir well and cook for another 2 minutes. Remove the pan from the heat and stir in the vinegar and parsley. Leave to cool for a few minutes.

Tip the mixture into a food processor and pulse until you have a smoother consistency, but not too smooth – you want to have a little bit of texture in the pâté. Transfer to one large or two small serving bowls and put in the fridge to cool completely.

If you would like to serve the pâté at a later date, put a thyme sprig on the top of each pâté and pour a thin layer of melted butter over the top, then put in the fridge to set until needed. The pâté will keep for 4–5 days. Serve with thin slices of sourdough toast.

Variety is everything – it keeps us from getting bored so it's important to have a good selection of dips to choose from. Salsa verde is a complex mix of flavours and is bound to jazz up your tacos or be the best answer to your chip and dip.

SALSA Verde

SERVES 4

1 large handful of mint
   leaves, finely chopped
1 large handful of basil
   leaves, finely chopped
1 large handful of flat-leaf
   parsley leaves, finely
   chopped
1 large garlic clove,
   finely chopped
40g cornichons, finely chopped
1½ tbsp baby capers,
   finely chopped
1 tsp Dijon mustard
2 tbsp red wine vinegar
120ml extra virgin olive oil,
   plus extra for sealing
   (optional)
Sea salt and freshly ground
   black pepper

When chopping the herbs use a very sharp knife; don't be tempted to put the herbs through a food processor, because the blade will bruise them – as will a blunt knife.

Put the chopped herbs in a bowl and add the garlic, cornichons, capers, mustard, vinegar and the 120ml oil. Sprinkle with a little salt and pepper, and mix well. Put in a bowl to serve. Alternatively, if you would like to keep the salsa for 4–5 days, store it inside a screwtop jar and cover it with a thin layer of olive oil.

The combination of sweet and smoky flavours in this red pepper hummus is addictive! Perfect with some warm pitta bread (my go-to snack) or some crudités (if you're feeling extra healthy). This would also be lovely with some warm bread as a starter if you're having guests round for dinner.

Smoky Red Pepper HUMMUS

SERVES 4

1 tbsp olive oil
1 small onion, finely chopped
2 garlic cloves, thickly sliced
1 tsp smoked paprika, plus
    extra to garnish
150g roasted red peppers
    from a jar
400g can chickpeas,
    drained and rinsed
Juice of 1 lemon
1½ tbsp tahini
40ml extra virgin olive oil,
    plus 1 tbsp to garnish
40ml light olive oil
Salt and freshly ground
    black pepper
1 tsp finely chopped flat-leaf
    parsley leaves, to garnish

Heat the oil in a small frying pan over a medium heat. Add the onion and garlic, and cook for 8 minutes or until they are softened and beginning to brown. Stir in the smoked paprika and remove from the heat.

Put the onion mixture into a powerful blender or food processor. Add the peppers. Reserve 1 tbsp chickpeas for the garnish, and add the remainder to the blender. Add the lemon juice, tahini, and the oils. Season with salt and pepper, then blend until smooth.

Put into a bowl and make a dent in the centre. Pour in the 1 tbsp extra virgin olive oil and the reserved chickpeas. Sprinkle with parsley and smoked paprika.

INDEX

A BIG thank you to . . .

This book is so much more than I could have ever imagined it to be and it wouldn't have become a reality without the many great and hard-working people involved. My goal was to create a vegan cookbook that made people excited to be vegan and eat vegan food. I wanted to create a book that *I* would buy and treasure.

From the word go the team at Little, Brown (Rhiannon, Hannah, Stephie, Beth, Aimee, Tracey and Nithya) have exceeded my expectations, with their levels of creativity and organisation being somewhat overwhelming! Not only that, but managing to work alongside a team of such nice people was a dream come true.

From the first shoot day, when I arrived to a location and props I'd only dreamt of, everything was on point thanks to the team at Whitefox and, in particular, Annabel Wright. When the first photo came out I knew straight away that no changes needed to be made and no criticism was worthy. The photos Mike English took are beautiful and thank you to Nicole Herft for working with me on the recipes, and for the food styling, as well as to Sarah Birks for the props—everything was so in sync with all the wonderful images and amazingly efficient.

I'd also like to thank my hair and make-up team, Summer Dyason and Lamphane from Michael Van Clarke. Not only did they have me looking my best, but they were great food dummies who revelled in the recipe tasting, showering the food with praise! Not to mention Summer going above and beyond and actually taking part in some of the shots.

None of this would have been possible if it wasn't for my amazing team at United Agents who saw my vision from the beginning, believed this could become a reality and did everything they could to make it happen. So thank you Matt Nicholls, Ariella Feiner and Harry Carlile for always hearing out my ideas and dreams.

Last but not least I'd like to thank my family and friends for supporting me always and trying out all the recipes – without fail they were ready with a compliment for the food. In particular my sister Tiffany, mother Fiona and bestie Marika who join me in celebrating veganism and keep me uplifted in every part of this movement. And, of course, my boyfriend James for putting up with (slash: massively enjoying) my non-stop cooking at home, giving me valuable feedback every step of the way.

Without everyone involved, this book wouldn't have been possible and I can't thank you enough.

SPHERE

First published in Great Britain in 2017 by Sphere

Recipe Concepts Originated by Lucy Watson
Recipe Writing, Development and Food Styling: Nicole Herft
Photography: Mike English
Props Styling: Sarah Birks
Book Design: Anna Green at siulendesign.com
Frames p6–7 and images p8–9 all © Shutterstock
Make-up: Summer Dyason
Clothes Styling: Hannah Beck
Hair: Lamphane at Michael Van Clarke
Select props, including the wall art on page 190, from Oliver Bonas, with thanks
Project management by whitefox

3 5 7 9 10 8 6 4 2

A CIP catalogue record for this book is available from the British Library.

ISBN 978-0-7515-6859-2

Printed in Germany.
Papers used by Sphere are from well-managed forests and other responsible sources.

Sphere
An imprint of
Little, Brown Book Group
Carmelite House
50 Victoria Embankment
London EC4Y 0DZ

An Hachette UK Company
www.hachette.co.uk

www.littlebrown.co.uk